CRICKET

CROWOOD SPORTS GUIDES

CRICKET

TECHNIQUE • TACTICS •TRAINING

Doug Ferguson

The Crowood Press

First published in 1992 by
The Crowood Press Ltd
Ramsbury, Marlborough
Wiltshire SN8 2HR

British Library Cataloguing in Publication Data

A catalogue record for this book is available from the British Library.

ISBN 1 85223 600 0

Acknowledgements

Photographs from Allsport, except those on pages 18 and 19, which are reproduced
by kind permission of Gray-Nicholls.
Demonstrations by Brian Lander, Durham City CC; David Wilson, Chester le Street
CC; Geoffrey Robinson, Tynemouth CC.
Thanks to K. V. Andrew, Chief Executive, National Cricket Association, for writing the
foreword; to Fosia Ali, Senior Physiotherapist, Washington Hospital, for her advice on
first aid; and to Durham City CC for use of their cricket field; also to Stanley Paul &
Co. Ltd; Hamlyn Publishing Group; and New Zealand Cricket Inc. Special thanks go to
Ken Ferguson and Ian Ferguson for their help with reading the manuscript and proofs.

Throughout this book the pronouns 'he', 'him' and 'his' have been used inclusively and
are intended to apply to both males and females.

Typeset by Chippendale Type Ltd, Otley, West Yorkshire.
Printed and bound in Great Britain by BPCC Hazells Ltd,
Member of BPCC Ltd.

CONTENTS

PREFACE

Cricket, lovely cricket
At Lord's they are playing it. (Calypso)

Not just at Lord's though, but in many countries, throughout the world and in their major cities, towns and villages.

As in all other sports, winning is important but a cricketer can obtain satisfaction from many aspects of the game without necessarily being a star player. An important catch which rids the opposition of its best batsman, a magnificent stop which prevents a winning boundary, a brief not-out innings which saves a match: all these can bring a glow to a cricketer in the same way that a win brings a glow to the team as a whole.

Cricket is primarily a team game, however, and although individuals may play major roles in winning a match, it is the combined efforts of the whole team which decides the outcome.

To play a successful part for your club it is necessary to have a reasonable skill level. Some of those skills are described and shown in Part 2, however, these skills must be practised, and the better players are those who can apply the skills under pressure – in other words, during a match situation.

FOREWORD

As I write this foreword to Doug Ferguson's excellent book I hope to find the words that will convey to readers, the essential character of a special man of cricket.

I first met Doug Ferguson in the 1970s when as NCA's Director of Coaching I needed to strengthen our coaching influence in the North East. I knew then of his reputation as a fine cricketer and league pro' of the old school. I had also heard that he held fairly strong views on how the game should be coached. In 1979 he applied for and was appointed NCA National Coach for the Northern Region. With respect to the other very capable applicants Doug had no opposition. His reputation had been well earned and his influence on the development of cricket coaching in this country should never go unrecognized. For the whole of the 1980s Doug Ferguson brought to the National Coaching Scheme many qualities. He wasn't the tough uncompromising character that I had imagined. In fact, he was and still is, a very likeable and sincere man with an open mind, who is constantly looking to develop his cricket coaching knowledge and ability. In cricket coaching terms Doug Ferguson will never be old as this book simply confirms.

Throughout Doug's career with the National Cricket Association he had a very close bond with the other National Coaches; Bob Carter, Bob Cottam, Les Lenham, Graham Saville and David Wilson, none of whom give praise easily. Every October on the afternoon before the Advanced Course at Lilleshall we played golf, greatly determined to win a rather special trophy. At first, not being a golfer, Doug didn't participate. Even when he eventually did, little success came his way and one could have thought he was destined to always hold the wooden spoon. We knew better however, as with much application he acquired a very practical swing and soon became the man to beat. Our only objection was the length of time he spent searching for his tee-peg!

This little story may tell you why, in addition to being recognised as a talent spotter supreme, he became one of the world's great if unsung, cricket coaches. I can think of a number of County and Test Match cricketers who were very fortunate to have crossed his path in their formative years.

'Cricket' will make a truly worthwhile contribution to cricket coaching literature. It combines a simplicity of style with typical Crowood clarity in presentation at a cost that should ensure a copy finding its way to every cricketer and coach worthy of the name.

Keith Andrew

PART I

INTRODUCTION

CHAPTER 1

AN EXPLANATION OF CRICKET

Cricket is an outdoor, fair-weather, summer game devised and developed by the English. Nowadays, it is played in many parts of the world by other countries who have been attracted by the game. The casual observer will find cricket difficult to understand, but a closer look will be rewarding.

The game is a contest between two opposing sides or teams each made up of eleven players. The players wear white shirts, trousers, socks, boots and sweaters. The club colours are often depicted in bands around the bottom of the sweater and sleeves. The game is played in the middle of a circular field, around the edge of which is a boundary line marking the limits of the playing area. The grass on the field is cut short, especially on the rectangle in the middle of the field which is known as the square. On this square the groundsman prepares the pitch for the game. This is a strip of ground 20m (22yd) long and about 2.75m (3yd) wide. The area outside the square is known as the outfield.

At each end of this playing strip is a wicket consisting of three wooden stumps 71cm (28in) above the ground, and these stumps are near enough to each other to prevent the ball from passing through them. The wicket is 23cm (9in) wide and is defended by the batsman against attack by the bowler who bowls the cricket ball from the other end of the pitch. The ball weighs 160g (5½oz), and each batsman uses a wooden cricket bat about 97cm (38in) long and 11cm (4½in) wide.

Before the game begins the two captains decide by the spin of a coin which side will bat first. The captain who calls correctly has the choice of arranging to bat first or of asking the opposing side to 'take first knock'. The game is conducted by two umpires (referees) who should be wise in the ways and laws of the game. One takes up position behind one of the wickets from which the bowling will commence, and the other stands about 20m (22yd) away from, and at right angles to, the other wicket. Each umpire has six counters in his pocket which are used to remind him when he is at the bowling end of the pitch to call 'over' after six lawful deliveries of the ball have been delivered. The fielding side, that is the side not batting first, will take to the field. One of their members wears leg-guards and gloves to protect himself from the ravages of the ball, and takes up position behind the stumps at the opposite end from the umpire who is standing behind the stumps – he is the wicket-keeper.

The two opening batsmen of the batting side then come on to the field to play. One batsman takes up his batting stance in front of the wicket behind which the wicket-keeper crouches ready to catch the ball if the batsman misses. The batsman makes a mark on the white line (crease) which is 1.2m (4ft) in front of the stumps. This is known as 'taking his guard'. The captain of the fielding side has by now dispersed nine of his players including himself about the playing area to prevent the batsman scoring runs (points). The other two players are, of course, the wicket-keeper and the player chosen to be the bowler. When all is ready the umpire at the bowling end calls 'play'.

The bowler bowls a series of six deliveries called an 'over'. The umpire takes care to see that all of these deliveries are in accordance with the laws of the game. In the case of a bowler bowling an unfair delivery the umpire calls 'no ball', one run is added to the batsman's total and the bowler must bowl a legal delivery in its place. Runs are normally scored when the batsman hits the ball, the two batsmen run towards the opposite ends and cross over to make good their ground. Should one of the fielders catch the ball before it touches the ground the batsman's innings end. If the ball crosses the boundary line without touching the field, in other words, lands over the line when it is hit, then the batsman is awarded six runs. If it crosses the boundary line but has touched the ground then four runs are scored. A batsman who fails to score any runs is said to be out for a 'duck'.

Before continuing, let us look at the names given to some of the positions in the field where the captain of the fielding side may place his men. These names are mostly relative to the two halves of the ground divided by an imaginary line running down the middle of the pitch and extending to the boundary line at both ends. Look at Fig 1 the batsman who is being bowled to at any time is taking strike and is therefore called the 'striker'. The area of the field behind him as he stands facing the bowler is the leg-side or on-side. The opposite half of the field is called the off-side.

Basically in a match the team scoring the most runs is the winning side. The side which is batting tries to score runs; the fielding side attempts not only to prevent its opponents from scoring but also attempts to bring each batsman's innings to a close within the laws of the game. A draw can take place in a time-limited game when the side batting second fails to reach the total of the side batting first, but has not lost all of their wickets when time is called.

Laws

There are forty-two Laws of the Game with many sub-sections to each Law. It is

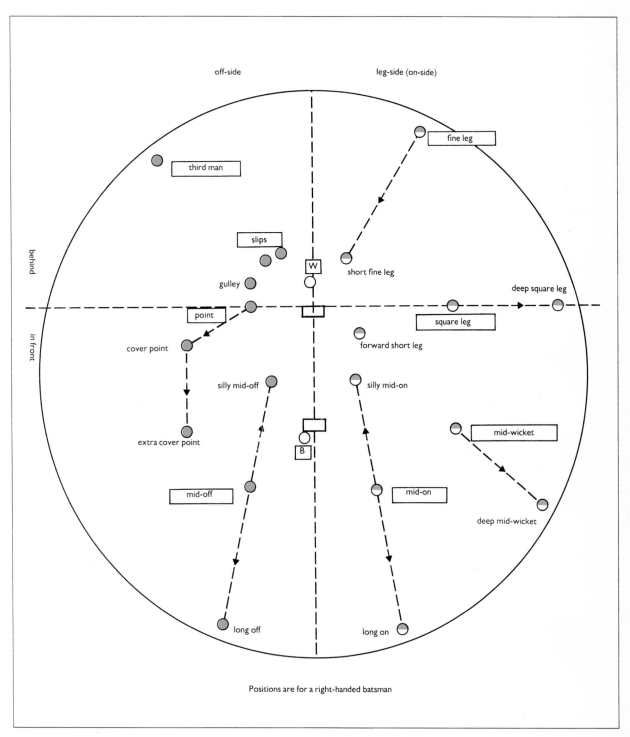

Fig 1   *There are only twenty fielding positions indicated here. Many variations can be made but only nine fielders can be used!*

much too difficult to explain all of the Laws, but some of the essential rules are outlined below.

Ways of Getting Out

Bowled out – Law 30.
Timed out – Law 31.
Caught out – Law 32.
Handling the ball – Law 33.
Hitting the ball twice – Law 34.
Hitting the wicket – Law 35.
Leg before wicket – Law 36.
Obstructing the field – Law 37.
Run out – Law 38.
Stumped – Law 39.

The most contentious law as far as cricketers are concerned is leg before wicket (lbw). Bowlers often appeal for lbw, forgetting that they are not in line wicket to wicket so that they see the impact of the ball differently from the umpire. On

the other side, batsmen often feel aggrieved that they have been given out when they thought they were well forward, when in fact they had only taken a short pace forward.

Remember   Lbw decisions are made 'in the opinion of the umpire' and although umpires do make mistakes, *so do players!*

Law 36 Leg Before Wicket

1. **Out LBW**   The Striker shall be out lbw in the circumstances set out below:
(a) *Striker Attempting to Play The Ball*   The Striker shall be out lbw if he first intercepts with any part of his person, dress or equipment a fair ball which would have hit the wicket and which has not previously touched his bat or a hand holding the bat, provided that: (i) The ball pitched, in a straight line between wicket and wicket or on the off side of the

Striker's wicket, or was intercepted full pitch; and (ii) the point of impact is in a straight line between wicket and wicket, even if above the level of the bails.
(b) *Striker Making No Attempt To Play The Ball*   The Striker shall be out lbw even if the ball is intercepted outside the line of the off-stump, if, in the opinion of the Umpire, he has made no genuine attempt to play the ball with his bat, but has intercepted the ball with some part of his person and if the other circumstances set out in (a) above apply.

Laws Affecting Bowlers

No ball – Law 24.
Bowler unable to finish his over – Law 17.
Bowlers changing ends – Law 22(5).
The bowling of wides – Law 25.
Aspects of unfair play – Law 42.

Earlier in this section I mentioned the ways that a batsman can get out – obviously some of these also affect bowlers, for example, Laws 30, 32, 35, 36 and 39. However, of all the laws affecting bowlers, the one that causes the greatest amount of misunderstanding is no ball.

Law 24 No Ball

1. **Mode of Delivery**   The Umpire shall indicate to the Striker whether the Bowler intends to bowl over or round the wicket, overarm or underarm, or right or left-handed. Failure on the part of the Bowler to indicate in advance a change in his mode of delivery is unfair and the Umpire shall call and signal a 'no ball'.
2. **Fair Delivery – The Arm**   For a delivery to be fair the ball must be bowled not thrown – see Note (a) below. If either

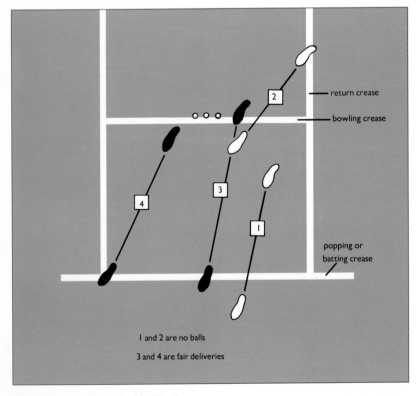

return crease

bowling crease

popping or batting crease

I and 2 are no balls

3 and 4 are fair deliveries

Fig 2   Examples of fair and unfair deliveries.

Umpire is not entirely satisfied with the absolute fairness of a delivery in this respect he shall call and signal 'no ball' instantly upon delivery.

3. Fair Delivery – The Feet   The Umpire at the bowler's wicket shall call and signal 'no ball' if he is not satisfied that in the delivery stride:
(a) the Bowler's back foot has landed within and not touching the return crease or its forward extension
or
(b) some part of the front foot whether grounded or raised was behind the popping crease.

4. Bowler Throwing at Striker's Wicket Before Delivery   If the Bowler, before delivering the ball, throws it at the Striker's wicket in an attempt to run him out, the Umpire shall call and signal 'no ball'. See Law 42.12. (Batsman Unfairly Stealing a Run) and Law 38. (Run Out.)

5. Bowler Attempting to Run Out Non-Striker Before Delivery   If the Bowler, before delivering the ball, attempts to run out the non-Striker, any runs which result shall be allowed and shall be scored as no balls. Such an attempt shall not count as a ball in the over. The Umpire shall not call 'no ball'. See Law 42.12 (Batsman Unfairly Stealing a Run).

6. Infringement of Laws by a Wicket-Keeper or a Fieldsman   The Umpire shall call and signal 'no ball' in the event of the Wicket-Keeper infringing Law 40.1. (Position of Wicket-Keeper) or a Fieldsman infringing Law 41.2. (Limitation of On-side Fieldsmen) or Law 41.3. (Position of Fieldsmen.)

7. Revoking a Call   An Umpire shall revoke the call 'no ball' if the ball does not leave the Bowler's hand for any reason. See Law 23.2. (Either Umpire Shall Call and Signal 'Dead Ball'.)

8. Penalty   A penalty of one run for a no ball shall be scored if no runs are made otherwise.

9. Runs From a No Ball   The Striker may hit a no ball and whatever runs result shall be added to his score. Runs made otherwise from a no ball shall be scored no balls.

10. Out From a No Ball   The Striker shall be out from a no ball if he breaks Law 34. (Hit the Ball Twice) and either Batsman may be Run Out or shall be given out if either breaks Law 33. (Handled the Ball) or Law 37. (Obstructing the Field.)

11. Batsman Given Out Off a No Ball   Should a Batsman be given out off a no ball the penalty for bowling it shall stand unless runs are otherwise scored.

NOTES
(a) Definition of a Throw
A ball shall be deemed to have been thrown if, in the opinion of either Umpire, the process of straightening the bowling arm, whether it be partial or complete, takes place during that part of the delivery swing which directly precedes the ball leaving the hand. This definition shall not debar a Bowler from the use of the wrist in the delivery swing.
(b) No Ball not Counting in Over
A no ball shall not be reckoned as one of the over. See Law 22.3. (No Ball or Wide Ball.)

The laws of the game reproduced here are printed by kind permission of MCC. Copies of the current edition of *The Laws of Cricket*, with full notes and interpretations, can be obtained from MCC at Lord's Cricket Ground, London NW8 8QN.

The Scores

It is the responsibility of the umpires to see to the correctness of the scores, both throughout and at the end of the game.

CHAPTER 2

TYPES OF CRICKET

Cricket is played at different levels, varying with the standard of the players and with the amount of time they are prepared to devote to the game.

Afternoon Cricket

Afternoon cricket is the most widely spread form of the game and village cricket fields are a common sight all over England. The players belonging to such clubs usually play every Saturday afternoon in the summer against other similar clubs. Often these clubs are grouped into leagues and each club will play every other club in the league twice during the season – once at home and the other away. The competitive element in this class of cricket takes two forms: striving to become the top club in the league and also through entering knock-out competitions which allow them to retain a cup or trophy for one year.

In certain parts of England, the ambition to be a 'top' club has led to the clubs hiring professionals, either from overseas or using local talent. One may often see in a league game two of the world's leading overseas players in opposition.

County Cricket

First-class county cricket is played on a very different scale. Here we have large grounds, large pavilions, permanent provision for coaching and practice, and seating accommodation for many thousands of spectators. It requires both ability and character for a boy to prove himself acceptable as a player for a first-class county. It is a hard profession but a most enjoyable one with the players playing practically every day of the week during the season. County cricket is such a costly affair, with clubs having to pay the wages of the professional players, ground staff and administrative staff, that in recent years they have accepted sponsorship from insurance companies, whisky distillers, cigarette manufacturers and the like whose goods or services are advertised all around the ground. This has led to the first-class sides not only playing their normal three- and four-day games, but also a number of one-day matches of limited overs.

One-Day Cricket

In the early 1960s attendance levels at county cricket grounds dropped alarmingly and by the middle 1960s they had dropped even further. In an attempt to arrest the drop in people watching cricket and a more worrying drop in membership it was decided to inaugurate a sixty-overs competition – this was the first of the big sponsorship deals. The public took very much to this new game, deciding that it liked to see a match start and finish in the same day.

The Refuge Sunday League started in 1969. This is a forty-over-a-side game and again has proved profitable at the gate, but in many critics' eyes this 'forty-over slog' is detrimental to the development of cricketers. A further one-day competition for the counties, sponsored by Benson & Hedges commenced in 1972. This is a fifty-five over game and again is very popular with spectators and county treasurers.

There is no doubt that the one-day games have attracted spectators, brought much-needed revenue into the county circuit and provided a change from the normal three- or four-day county championship matches. There is also talk now of having the teams wearing coloured clothing to add to the spectacle of the one-day competitions.

The proliferation of the one-day games is further escalated by the one-day internationals now played whenever a touring side visits. The first one played took place in 1971 and was 'accidental'. It was arranged hurriedly when the Test Match at Melbourne between Australia and England was abandoned because of rain. The first One-Day World Cup played in England took place in 1975 and was won by the West Indies. This World Cup is now part of the cricket calendar and is played every four years.

Although the length of the innings in the one-day competition may vary, all the matches stipulate that there is a limitation on the number of overs that a bowler may bowl. There are fielding circles marked out in which a certain number of fielders must be at all times – this is to stop the practice of placing every fielder on the boundary.

The verdicts on one-day cricket are:
1. The public like it. They can see a result before their eyes, unlike a county championship where they have to watch for three days or a Test Match when they must watch for five days – even then the outcome may be a draw.
2. It provides much needed income, not just at the gate but through sponsorship and in many cases through television coverage.
3. Many feel that the type of cricket played with defensive fields and risky stroke manipulation does not lead to the development of Test cricketers, however, others feel that if the players are good enough they should be able to adapt.
4. Without doubt one-day cricket matches have improved the standard of fielding. Fielders chase and harry, and throw with accuracy and pace so that much of the fielding is a joy to watch.

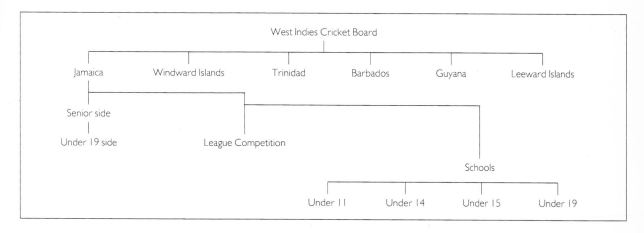

Test Cricket

The highest level of cricket is 'Test' cricket which is played between the major cricketing countries of the world – England, Australia, West Indies, India, Pakistan, New Zealand and Sri Lanka. These matches are played over five days and generally stimulate a tremendous amount of interest. In a five-match series with television coverage much needed finance is generated. In England a lot of this money is distributed to the counties, who in turn use some of the money for helping local cricket. A successful national side provides a stimulus for cricket throughout the rest of the country.

Cricket Outside England

West Indies

Cricket here is island-based, in other words, each of the six main island groups are responsible for their own organization. The six teams are Jamaica, Windward Islands, Trinidad, Barbados, Leeward Islands and Guyana.

Taking the island of Jamaica as an example, cricket in the schools is organized into four age groups – Under 11, Under 14, Under 15 and Under 19. At club level most clubs run three teams. At the Under-19 level there is representative cricket and there is an inter-island

competition (five games); this is the same at the Senior level.

The island coach is responsible for looking after the Under 19s and the Senior side, but there is very little organized coaching until players reach the Under-19 age group.

The inter-club games are very competitive but there is also a lot of soft-ball cricket played by all age groups on a casual basis – this impromptu cricket is even played sometimes with small, hard oranges with a 'fresh' one being used about every five overs!

Australia

The six states play in the Sheffield Shield and again are run independently, however, they are responsible to the Australian Cricket Board. The sides have similar types of organization and are Victoria, South Australia, New South Wales, Western Australia, Queensland and Tasmania.

In Victoria boys are picked when playing in their school sides to provide the basis of the Under-19 representative side. Coaching is available at some of the schools, and the state Under-19 side is the

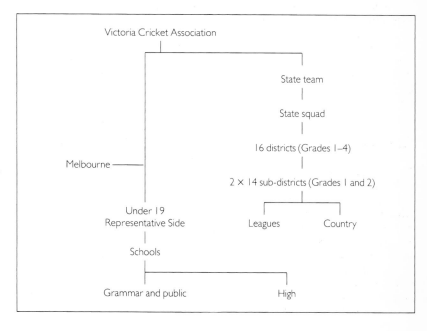

responsibility of the state coach.

The leagues and country clubs provide players for the sub-district and district sides. A state squad of about thirty players is then selected and a final sorting out provides the team to play in the Shell Shield Competition.

The following 'family tree' shows the detailed structure of cricket in Victoria.

New Zealand

The six provincial sides who play in their Shell Competition are Wellington, Central Districts, Canterbury, Northern Districts and Auckland.

Each province has a structure which is closely linked to the development at national level from the juniors at twelve, thirteen and fourteen years of age right through to the full New Zealand side. With these two programmes (shown on the flow chart) so nicely interwoven, it is possible for any youngster to see a clearly defined path to the top.

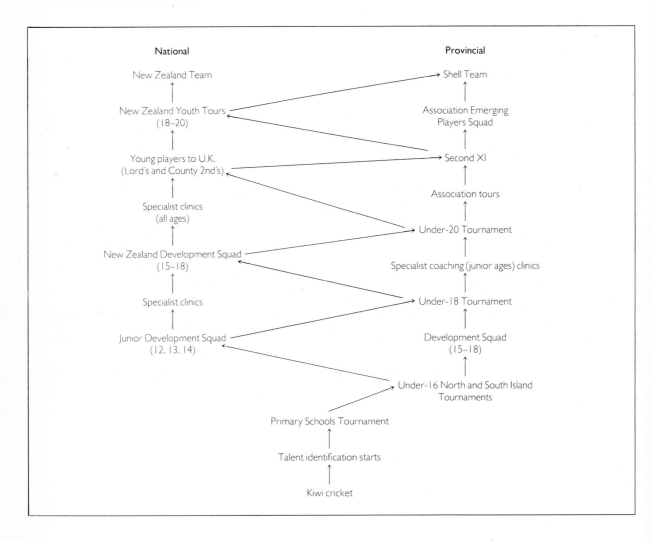

National	Provincial
New Zealand Team	Shell Team
New Zealand Youth Tours (18–20)	Association Emerging Players Squad
Young players to U.K. (Lord's and County 2nd's)	Second XI
Specialist clinics (all ages)	Association tours
New Zealand Development Squad (15–18)	Under-20 Tournament
Specialist clinics	Specialist coaching (junior ages) clinics
Junior Development Squad (12, 13, 14)	Under-18 Tournament
	Development Squad (15–18)
	Under-16 North and South Island Tournaments
Primary Schools Tournament	
Talent identification starts	
Kiwi cricket	

CHAPTER 3

CRICKET ETIQUETTE

'It's not cricket'

This expression has passed into the English language and has become a traditional way of denoting actions or behaviour which are unseemly, unfair, underhand and totally unacceptable. Some breaches of this sort of etiquette are examined later in this chapter.

There is perhaps no better definition of the game than some words from the monument to William Lillywhite who played in the 1840s, and who is said to have bowled no more than half a dozen wides in the whole of his cricketing life. His monument states:

Cricket is a sport in which the blessings of youthful strength and spirits may be most innocently enjoyed, to the exercise of the mind, the discipline of the temper, and the general improvement of the man.

From the saying 'It's not cricket', and asking ourselves what cricket is, we may infer from various examples what it is that comprises the etiquette of the game.

First and most obviously, we must set down clearly a basic rule which must be observed if unseemly examples of bad behaviour in the field are to be avoided – the rule, namely that umpires' decisions must be obeyed and done so without question. There must be no outward show of reluctance by a batsman to leave the crease on being given 'out', or by a bowler whose appeal for a catch or an lbw decision is turned down.

Umpires are charged with the running of a game (without umpires there is no game); a very difficult task when one thinks they may be called upon to act on any of the forty-two Laws of cricket. It is therefore up to captains and players to support the umpires, and not make things more difficult for them.

Players fielding within close earshot of the batsman must not make audible comments, especially with foul and abusive language, calculated to upset the batsman's concentration. This is commonly known as 'sledging' and is not needed in cricket.

Pre-arranged and concerted shouts of 'How's that' for an lbw decision or a bat-pad catch, and appeals by those in a poor position to see are totally against the spirit of the game.

Appealing for catches when the ball has been taken on the half-volley, lifting the seam of the ball with finger nails and deliberately wasting time are all examples of bad sportsmanship, a breach of etiquette and a thorough nuisance to the umpires involved.

What every cricketer knows in his heart to be fair and sportsmanlike is the basis of the spirit of the game. Cricket clubs acknowledge that there must be fair play in every department of the game and there have been very few examples of really bad behaviour. Hence our national proverb that what is not fair is 'not cricket'.

CHAPTER 4

EQUIPMENT

Cricket equipment can be quite costly and many clubs provide it for their players. Much of it may not suit a particular player – bats might be too heavy, pads too big and so on. Ideally it is best if a player has his own set of gear which he can care for and maintain himself.

Age	Size of bat	Weight of bat	Length of bat
Under 9	4	0.71kg (1lb 9oz)	76cm (30in)
Under 11	5/6	0.96kg (2lb 2oz)	79–84cm (31–33in)
Under 13	6/Harrow	0.99kg (2lb 3oz)	84–86cm (33–34in)
Under 15	Harrow/Full	1.02kg+ (2lb 4oz+)	86–89cm (34–35in)

A Bat

The maximum size for a bat is 96.5 × 11.5cm (38 × 4½in). It needs to be well balanced and not too heavy. A new bat which needs oiling (some do not) will need to be broken in by hitting an old cricket ball continuously or by hitting the bat with a mallet which has half a cricket ball fixed to the end. Be careful about overoiling the bat and using it against a cheap, hard ball.

To have a long or a short handle? Generally tall people use bats with a longer handle, but whatever feels right is the one to go for. There is a tendency nowadays to have more than one rubber grip on the handle – it is alleged that the ball can be driven further – but if you buy a bat like this make sure that your hands are large enough to cope with the extra thickness.

Selecting a Bat for Young Cricketers

In trying to give good advice for the selection of bats for young players one has to take into account the age, height, physique and strength. In recent years there has been a trend towards heavier and thicker bats for adults, and children are great copiers. However, I think that young cricketers should be discouraged from using these heavier bats until they are at least strong enough. A well-balanced bat which picks up easily with the top hand is much more appropriate for a growing child.

A rough-and-ready guide for the length of a bat is that when resting against the trousers the handle should not protrude past the bottom of the trouser pocket. The above recommendations on bat size are all approximate.

> **KIT CHECK**
>
> Old-fashioned batting pads were often too heavy and cumbersome and made quick running between the wickets a real chore. The more modern, lightweight pads help with this aspect of play. Pads with Velcro fastenings instead of the buckles can prevent chafing.

Batting Pads

These should feel comfortable and light enough so as not to hinder running between the wickets. The type of fasteners, buckles or Velcro is again personal choice: choose whichever does the job to your satisfaction. Do make sure that the pads are firm enough to resist a fast bowler's deliveries.

Boots and Shoes

If you are a medium to fast bowler you might possibly be better off having cricket

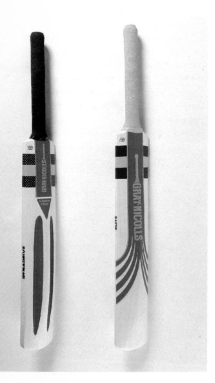

Fig 3 Your cricket bat should be well balanced and not too heavy.

> **KEY POINT**
>
> Pick the bat up with your top hand only – if you can pick it up easily it is probably the right size for you.

Fig 4   Batting pads should be light and comfortable.

boots which give good ankle support. Whichever you choose make sure that they are studded, preferably with metal spikes for bowlers. In dry, firm conditions those with dimpled rubber soles are fine for fielding and batting.

Batting Gloves

Research into the development of better batting gloves is continuous. It is certainly essential to wear well-made gloves with good padding on the parts of the hands facing the bowler.

Fig 5   Good batting gloves are an essential.

Abdominal Protector

Wearing a box is essential to prevent serious damage. It is easily slipped into a jockstrap which has a pouch for the purpose.

Thigh Pads

The upper front leg is very vulnerable to being hit and it certainly helps to have protection for it. It is possible nowadays to buy shorts which have a large pocket for the front thigh pad and a smaller pocket for the pad used to protect inside of the back leg.

Helmet

The increase of short-pitched bowling has led to an increase in the number of batsmen wearing a protective helmet. If by wearing a helmet a batsman feels more secure and safe, then he should wear one. Wearing a vizor or grid is very much a personal choice.

Wicket-Keeping Pads and Gloves

The modern lightweight, shortened pads are ideal to help wicket-keepers with their mobility and speed. Some gloves have a web between the thumb and forefinger and this can be a big help in catching the ball. It is most important that the gloves are supple and that they fit comfortably – by wearing inner gloves you can improve comfort considerably.

KEY POINT

In a hot, dry season when the ground becomes hard, there is great strain on the feet. Blisters can be most uncomfortable, so it is advisable to wear clean, thick socks which are well dusted on the inside with talcum powder. Always carry a spare pair of socks as a change can be quite refreshing.

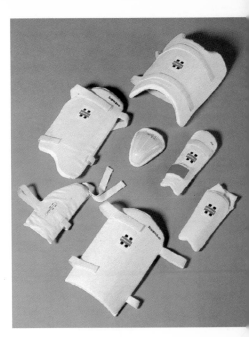

Fig 6   Protective equipment.

Shirts and Trousers

If they are too tight there is a restriction of movement and in hot weather this becomes most uncomfortable. Bowlers in particular, should wear T-shirts or undervests to protect their perspiring bodies from the effects of cooling down too quickly. They should wear one at the end of the day as well to protect their backs from chills.

Sweaters

Too often cricket is played on cold days and it is crucial that sweaters, long sleeved and sleeveless, are part of a cricketer's standard equipment. It is not only fielders who need them to keep warm, but the bowlers also require them at the end of their spell of bowling and between overs.

Extra Equipment

After a long day in the field or having played a long innings, a shower or bath can help revive tired limbs, so a towel, soap and talcum powder for the feet should always be in the club cricketer's bag.

PART 2
SKILLS AND TECHNIQUES

CHAPTER 5

BOWLING

It is essential that bowling is taught and learned early on so that batsmen can play strokes – if the ball is nowhere near the batsman he will be unable to hit the ball.

What requirements are needed for bowling?

1. A correct grip.
2. An economical run-up without any hiccups or stutters.
3. A high bowling arm as part of a well-balanced position at the crease.
4. A fluent and positive follow-through.

Every type of bowler needs to have rhythm and purpose from the beginning of

---

STAR TIP

Remember that the run-up is not an exercise in flamboyance, but simply a method of transport to get the body to the wicket in rhythm and in the correct bowling position.

Gary Sobers

---

the run-up to the end of the follow-through.

Basic Grip

A basic grip is to hold the ball with your first two fingers placed on either side of the seam and with your thumb on the seam underneath the ball (*see* Fig 7). Aim to have a gap in the 'V' between your first finger and the thumb. Do not hold the ball down in the palm of your hand.

Fig 9   This bowler's body is starting to turn from a good 'bound'.

Fig 10   For the delivery keep your back foot parallel to the crease. Your body should be leaning away from the batsman, with your front arm positioned upwards and backwards.

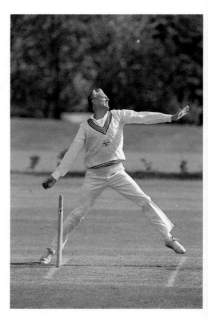

Fig 11   This is a good delivery stride for the pace. The bowler's head is looking along his extended front arm.

Fig 7   The basic grip. Keep your first two fingers on either side of the seam, with your thumb underneath and on the seam.

Fig 8   Note the clear gap with the ball held far up the fingers, but still held with control.

> **KEY POINT**
>
> Hold the ball as far up your fingers as you can while still feeling that you have control of it.

Run-Up

A bowler needs a run-up as this will enable him to bowl balls at the speed he desires for some considerable time. The exception is the fast bowler who generally needs to bowl in shorter spells. It is critical, therefore, that the length of the run-up is long enough to achieve good rhythm and balance. Make sure that when you practise you mark out your run-up and that you start from this spot all the time.

> **KEY POINT**
>
> Be clear in your mind what type of delivery you are going to bowl before setting off on your run-up.

During the run-up your body should face the batsman and when you bowl the ball your body turns sideways. To achieve this 90-degree turn it is necessary to 'bound' into the air and turn. This movement is done in the stride before the delivery stride (see Fig 9).

> **KIT CHECK**
>
> Make sure that your boots are in good condition and that they fit comfortably. Check that the spikes are long enough to stop you from slipping when the run-up is damp.

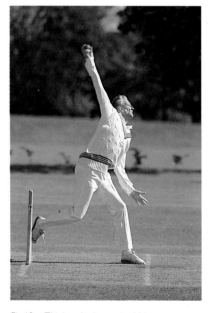

Fig 12   This bowler has a nice high bowling arm with the other arm coming down by his left side.

Fig 13   The good extension of both the bowler's arms shows maximum effort. His eyes are looking down the pitch.

Delivery

Having achieved a successful bound the bowler should aim to land with his back foot parallel to the crease and his body leaning back, away from the batsman. The ball should be close to his mouth, his front arm should be positioned both upwards and backwards and he should be looking over his front shoulder (see Fig 10). The bowler's body is now completely wound up like a coiled spring and is ready to be released, whilst his mind is concentrating on where he wants to pitch the ball.

As the bowler's front arm starts forward towards the stumps and his bowling arm commences its swing, the bowler takes his delivery stride with his front foot landing in line with the back foot but pointing roughly to the long leg (see Fig 11).

KEY POINT

Problems in your delivery stride:

1. If it is too long there is a loss of height.
2. If it is too short there is a danger of you losing your balance.
3. If your front foot lands too wide to the off-side thus opening up your body, there is a danger that the ball might be bowled down the leg-side.

The bowler's front knee lands and flexes, and then straightens (the faster the bowler the more it flexes). Right through the bowling action it is necessary to keep your eyes looking down the pitch.

It is essential to bowl with a high bowling arm. If you are playing in perfect batting conditions on a perfect batting pitch where there is no movement of the ball in the air or off the pitch, a high bowling arm may produce bounce which is one of the greatest difficulties a batsman can face (see Fig 12).

RULES CHECK

Be clear in your mind that you understand where your feet should be when delivering the ball, if you do not want to be called for a no ball (see Law 24(3)), page 13).

Follow-Through

The non-bowling arm should pass close to the body and then swing back and beyond it. The bowling arm should come across the body towards the left hip (see Fig 13).

Law 42 (Note c) states that the bowler is not allowed to run on the pitch.

KEY POINT

Bowling no balls can cause a problem. It often occurs if the creases are not marked out before practising starts or the bowler does not mark out his run-up. An inconsistent stride pattern then emerges and the bowler overstrides the crease. By using a video camera for six to ten balls and then running the tape through slowly it is usually easy to spot where the irregularities occur.

However, he does not want to turn off too quickly either as if he does so he will be in danger of losing his body action and balance.

Fig 14   Richard Hadlee after completing a delivery. Note how well he finishes his action off.

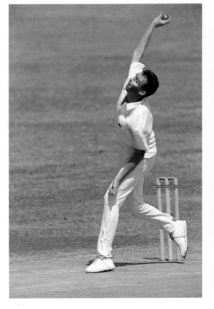

Fig 15   Angus Fraser bowling from close to the stumps and on his way to taking 5 for 29 versus West Indies.

STAR TIP

Bowl from close to the stumps.
Angus Fraser (Middlesex and England)

There have always been exceptions to the normal action and many successful Test bowlers have not conformed to all of the basics, for example, Bob Willis, Mike Proctor, Colin Croft and so on, but they have all been able to bowl straight. There are a good number of club bowlers, however, who do not have a good basic action and cannot consistently bowl straight. It might be as well for these bowlers to adhere to some of the principles laid down, particularly the one relating to having the front foot in line with the back foot even if it does not point to the long leg.

Swing Bowling

Away-Swinger

This occurs when bowling to a right-handed batsman – the ball swings in the air towards the slips. There are slight differences from the basic grip: the inside of the thumb lies along the seam and although the first two fingers are on either side of the seam, the seam is angled towards the slips (*see* Fig 17).

Make sure that the polished side of the

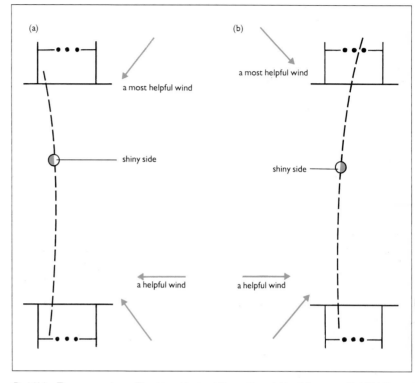

Fig 16(a)   The away-swinger. The shiny side should be on the outside of the curve. Fig 16(b) The in-swinger. The shiny side should be on the outside of the curve with the curve in towards the batsman.

> **KEY POINT**
>
> In the away-swinger:
>
> 1.   The bowling arm is high and the wrist quite firm, with the fingers behind the ball on release.
> 2.   The ball is bowled from close to the stumps.
> 3.   The body is kept sideways for as long as possible.
> 4.   The front foot is placed slightly across the crease to the leg-side, and the bowling arm follows through across the body.

ball (usually the side with the least printing on) is on the outside of the curve (*see* Fig 16).

In-Swinger

This time the ball swings in the air from off to leg. The grip used is with the pad of the thumb placed underneath the ball and the seam angled towards the leg slip (*see* Fig 18). The more polished side of the ball is again on the outside of the curve but

> **KEY POINT**
>
> For the in-swinger it helps if:
>
> 1.   The front foot is placed slightly to the off-side, thus opening the body up.
> 2.   The bowling arm is very high and follows through to the right leg.

Fig 17   The away-swinger. The seam should be angled towards the slips.

Fig 18   The in-swinger. The seam should be angled towards the leg slip.

this time the curve is towards the batsman (see Fig 16).

To give the ball the best chance to swing it must be pitched up – this makes the batsman play forward. The line to bowl, as Paul Allot infers in the Star Tip, is around the off stump.

Bowlers also need to have an alternative type of delivery which looks similar in grip to the stock ball they bowl.

Off-Cutter

This is the main variation for the away-swing bowler. On a dusty pitch or a drying one, the off-cutter can be a match-winner.

Grip the ball as for an away-swinger and then move the fingers so that the index finger lies on the seam (see Fig 19). On delivery pull the seam clockwise; this will impart spin. Unlike the off-spinner (see page 27) no use is made of the wrist.

Leg-Cutter

This is the main alternative delivery to the in-swinger. Grip the ball as for the in swing and then move the fingers so that the middle finger is on the seam (see Fig 20). When bowling, the middle finger pulls the seam in an anti-clockwise direction. Place the thumb on the off-side of the seam so that it can push the ball in the opposite direction to the middle finger.

Seam Bowling

Generally done, as for swing bowling, by the medium-paced bowlers. The seam bowler depends on:

1.   His ability to hit the pitch with the seam vertical.
2.   The pitch itself for help – if it is slightly damp with a fair amount of grass, the ball stands a chance of changing direction on impact.
3.   Varying the position of his wrist when delivering the ball.

One famous Yorkshire and England bowler was once asked to say how he bowled his 'inners' (off-cutters) and his 'outers' (leg-cutters). He replied, 'I don't know, but if I don't, neither does the b . . . . y batsman!'

Practice is needed to become a successful seam or swing bowler. As medium pacers are not fast enough to 'blast' batsmen out, it is essential that they bowl with accuracy and variety. Variations can be caused by:

1.   Bowling from different positions on the crease.
2.   Moving the position of the seam in the fingers.
3.   Varying the bowling speed.
4.   Using the wind.

The grip for seam bowling is the standard basic grip. It is advantageous to experiment with different wrist positions when releasing the ball.

Fig 19   The off-cutter. The index finger imparts cut, or spin, by pulling the seam clockwise.

Fig 20   The leg-cutter. The middle finger lies on the seam with the thumb at the side.

Fast Bowling

Having genuine, natural pace is a rarity and generally it has to be nurtured. Physical fitness is a prerequisite if a fast bowler is to remain fast and it helps the longevity of his career if he has a sound, basic action. However, as long as the bowler achieves real pace and good direction easily, the quality of his action is not too critical (*see* Fig 21).

Physical fitness can be achieved and maintained with a combination of:

1.   Regular bowling.
2.   Adherence to a fitness programme.
3.   A proper diet.
4.   A determination to bowl fast.

Spin Bowling

This is a most difficult art in which to achieve success. To be a successful spinner requires:

1.   The ability to spin the ball.
2.   The ability to 'flight' the ball.
3.   Patience.
4.   A strong mental attitude.
5.   Good control of line and length.

In local cricket a lot of cricket fields are not very large and the spinner can often be mishit for a four or six. Even with a well-placed field setting, the spinner is at a disadvantage because of the smallness of the playing area. Nevertheless it is important that spinners keep on practising and are encouraged to learn the art of spin bowling. It is often said that you do not become a good spinner until you reach the age of thirty!

Off-Spinner

In this case the ball turns in to a right-handed batsman.

The ball is held between the first two fingers with the seam at right angles to them (*see* Figs 22(a) and (b)). The further apart the fingers can be spaced with comfort, the greater the leverage that can be applied by the index finger – the main spinning ingredient. The ball is spun clockwise on delivery and the thumb plays no part in the spinning of the ball.

Another useful grip, particularly for those with shorter fingers, is achieved by placing the first finger alongside the seam, with the second finger spread comfortably apart. The first finger exerts spin by being wedged against the seam (*see* Fig 23) and

Fig 21   Graham Dilley (Kent) approaching the wicket.

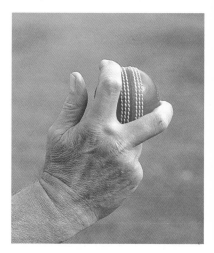

Fig 22(a) and (b)   The off-spinner.
(a) An orthodox grip – the thumb is
off the ball.

Fig 22(b)   A different view of the
orthodox off-spinner grip showing the
wide spread of the fingers.

Fig 23   The off-spinner – an
alternative grip. This grip is useful
when the ball is turning too much.

the whole action is the same as with the orthodox grip. This grip is also very useful on a turning pitch when you do not want to spin the ball too much.

Floater

This is an essential part of the successful off-spinner's repertoire. The grip is very similar to the second grip mentioned for the off-spinner, except that the first finger now lies on the seam (see Fig 26), and instead of pulling the first finger down, it stays behind the ball and pushes the ball towards the off stump.

One other variation is to undercut the ball and this sometimes has the effect of

KEY POINT

For the off-spinner it helps if:

1.   The delivery stride is short with the front knee slightly across to the leg-side and braced a little (see Fig 24).
2.   The right knee is brought up enabling the bowler to feel 'tall' (see Fig 25).
3.   The follow-through of the arms is vigorous.

Fig 24   The delivery stride for the off-spinner should be short with a braced front knee.

Fig 25   A high right knee keeps the bowler upright during the off-spinner and increases the possibility of more 'bounce'.

Fig 26   The floater – the index finger stays behind the ball on delivery.

Fig 27(a) and (b)   The leg spinner. (a) Note that the third finger on the seam is ready to give a final thrust.

Fig 27(b)   The view from mid-off.

causing the ball to spin in the air *towards* the slips, all the time giving the impression that it is an off break. No wonder it takes a long time to become a first-class spin bowler!

Leg-Spinner

In this case the ball turns away from a right-handed batsman.

The ball is held basically in the first two fingers, which are not spread as wide as for an off-spinner, with the third finger bent and lying along the seam. The base of the thumb acts as a support (*see* Fig 27(a)). The wrist is bent inwards and then flips forward anti-clockwise so that the third finger gives the ball the final thrust (*see* Fig 27(b)). A high bowling arm gives the

KEY POINT

For the leg-spinner it helps if:

1.   The delivery stride is across to the leg-side, but is longer than for an off-spinner.
2.   The height of the bowling arm is varied so that the flight variations can be achieved.

chance of more bounce and again the action must be 'finished off' as normal.

Googly

This is the leg-spinner's alternative ball which spins into a right-handed batsman. The ball is held in exactly the same way as for the leg break. However, when the leg break is bowled the back of the wrist faces mid-off, but when the googly is bowled the back of the wrist faces the batsman, again

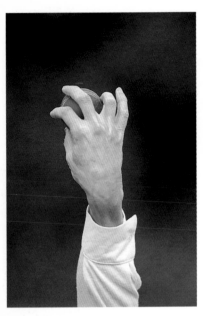

Fig 28   The googly – a view from the batting end. The back of the hand is facing down the pitch.

with the third finger being the last to touch the ball (see Fig 28).

The less change there is in the action, the greater the chances are of deceiving the batsman. Because wrist spin is more difficult to control than finger spin, there is a reluctance in some club cricket to persevere with leg-spinners.

KEY POINT

For the googly it helps if:

1.   The body is slightly open – place the front foot to the off-side of the straight.
2.   The front shoulder is dropped slightly.
3.   The bowling arm follows through to the right leg.

Left-Arm Bowling

The basic principles of the bowling action apply equally to right- and left-handed

---

STAR TIP

To right-handed batsmen I aim to bowl middle to middle and off so that both the leg break and the googly have a chance of taking a wicket. Occasionally I aim to bowl it a little wider so making the batsman reach for it. To left-handed batsmen I sometimes bowl round the wicket, especially if there is a rough area outside the left-hander's off stump. Lots of spin on the ball sometimes makes the ball dip.

Michael Atherton
(Lancashire and England)

---

bowlers. There are some differences, however, in the application of the skills.

Fast and Medium Bowling

More often than not the line of attack is from over the wicket, at the middle and off stumps. By choosing this line the bowler presents the batsman with two problems:

1.   Basically he will be bowling from leg to off with his natural swing bringing the ball into the right-handed batsman.
2.   If the ball does not swing it will be going away from the batsman, who may then play inside the line of the ball.

Spin

The slow, left-arm spinner does in fact mirror the off-spinner in the basic principles of grip, run-up, delivery and follow-through. He will nearly always bowl from around the wicket. As he turns the ball away from the right-handed batsman he therefore poses a different set of problems than the off-spinner.

Useful Hints

1.   When a pitch is 'green', in other words, when the grass has not been cut too short, it usually presents ideal conditions for seam bowlers. The depth of grass gives the ball a chance to 'bite' and deviate off the seam.
2.   On slower pitches medium-paced bowlers are often very difficult to score off and can be more effective than quicker bowlers.
3.   When the pitch is drying out after rain or the top is crumbling because it is too dry, then spinners or bowlers who can cut the ball will usually be the ones who are liable to bowl a side out.
4.   Against batsmen who like to swing the bat freely the bowler has to try and deny them room. It is no good bowling outside the off stump; the aim should be to pitch the ball right in at the batsman's feet.
5.   To counteract the batsman who is reluctant to play shots or is playing for a draw, spin bowlers might have the best chance of getting him out. By giving the ball 'plenty of air', by varying the amount of spin and by constantly bowling from different positions at the crease it might be

Fig 29   Phil Edmonds (Middlesex) bowling against India at Delhi, with some attacking close fielders.

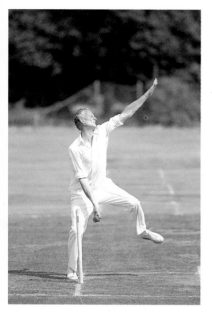

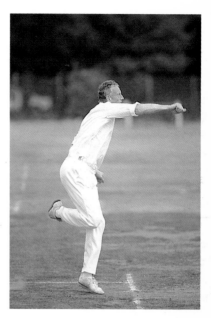

Fig 30   The front arm has not gone back far enough and the bowler is unable to get much 'body' into his action.

Fig 31   The bowling arm is not very high here so the bowler would not get much bounce.

Fig 32   A poor follow-through of the bowling arm when bowling off-spinners will mean a lack of 'bite'.

possible to lure the batsman into playing a false shot.

6.   At all times, whatever the state of the pitch, the genuine fast bowler has a chance of taking a wicket. Sheer speed can surprise even the best of batsmen. When the ball is new he will make the ball bounce more. The quick bowler can also be used to advantage against a new batsman in the middle of an innings and against the tail-enders.

7.   Swing bowling – reverse swing. As described earlier, to swing a ball the shiny side is normally on the outside of the curve as it has less wind resistance than the other side. When the ball has lost its newness and is roughed up a little it is possible to add moisture (sweat) to the side which is

the least rough to make the ball swing the other way. The theory is that by adding moisture the ball is then heavier on that side and the ball therefore swings to the wet side.

Possible Faults

1.   Having the wrong grip for the intended type of delivery.

2.   Having too long a run-up can mean loss of balance, lack of power at the crease and inability to bowl for long spells.

3.   Having too short a run-up does not give a bowler time to achieve rhythm and 'gather' himself.

4.   Poor use of the front arm can make

for a poor body action and lack of impetus.

5.   By not picking up the front knee quicker bowlers will not achieve much lean-back when landing at the crease.

6.   If the bowling arm is not high there will be a resultant loss of bounce.

7.   Poor positioning of the front foot (too much to the off-side) can lead to the head falling away, thus causing the bowler to bowl down the leg-side.

8.   By not keeping the eyes looking at the target a poor line and length may be bowled.

9.   A poor follow-through of both arms, in other words, not completing the action, leads to loss of power.

CHAPTER 6

BATTING

It is often said that bowlers win matches and batsmen save them. As with all sayings there is a large element of truth in this – for example, in a lot of club games, bowlers have to bowl sides out to win. However, with the advent of overs matches bowlers often just bowl to contain batsmen and the onus is then on the batsmen to break the stranglehold of the bowlers.

Where do you start? With grip, stance and backlift as if you can get these fundamentals right you stand a good chance of playing strokes correctly.

Fig 33   Gripping the bat. The hands should be together with the bottom hand placed just below the centre of the handle.

Fig 34   Batting stance. The head is still with the eyes level and the body looking very comfortable.

Grip

Your hands should be together, as if they are apart on the handle they will often work against each other. Make sure that your thumbs and fingers are around the handle, with the Vs formed by the thumbs and forefingers in line and pointing between the outside edge and centre of the bat. Place your bottom hand just in the bottom half of the handle. (*See* Fig 33).

Stance

When standing at the crease keep one foot on either side of the crease and, depending on your height, about 8–15cm (3–6in) apart. The taller you are the wider apart your feet should be. Your knees should be slightly bent with your front shoulder directed at the bowler, your head still and your eyes level (*see* Fig 34). It may be necessary as you get older to hold the bat 5–8cm (2–3in) off the ground in order to keep your eyes level. If you rest the bat on your back toe it will lift you up and make you feel taller.

KEY POINT

It is often a help to left-handed batsmen if they keep their back foot parallel to the crease and open up their front foot slightly. This helps them to play straighter at the ball when it is bowled from the edge of the crease (over the wicket) by predominantly in-swing bowlers.

To complete a comfortable stance let your hands rest lightly on the inside of your front thigh, so that the back of your top hand faces roughly in the extra-cover/mid-off area.

Figs 35(a) and (b)   The backlift.

Fig 35(a)   Take the bat back straight over the stumps.

Fig 35(b)   The hands are nicely back and ready for action.

Backlift

Take the bat back and straight over the stumps with an open face. Leave a gap between the back elbow and the side of the body and keep the toe of the bat higher than the hands (*see* Figs 35(a) and (b)).

KEY POINT

During the backlift:

1.   Make sure that you keep your head still.
2.   Pick up the bat as the bowler's bowling arm starts its upward swing. If your backlift is too late your stroke may be hurried, and if it is too early there will be too much movement of the bat, especially if it is too heavy.

STAR TIP

When playing against very fast bowling look to play back, but be ready to play forward to score runs.

Michael Atherton
(Lancashire and England)

Back Play

More and more these days, because of the success of the West Indian fast bowlers, there is a tendency for the faster club

---

KIT CHECK

Select a bat which is not too heavy but which is nicely balanced. Make sure that you feel comfortable with it, no matter how long an innings you play.

---

bowlers to bowl just short of a length. It is necessary, therefore, to be able to defend well, particularly off the back foot.

Back Defence

This is played to a short-pitched ball which is pitching on or just outside the off stump.

1.   The back foot is taken back towards the stumps and kept parallel to the crease with the front shoulder just inside the line of the ball (*see* Fig 36(a)).
2.   Although the body-weight is nearly all on the back foot, the balance of the body is maintained by 'leaving the head behind'.
3.   The top hand keeps control of the bat assisted by a high front elbow (*see* Fig 36(b)).
4.   The bottom hand relaxes into a light thumb and forefinger grip only.

Figs 36(a)–(c)   Back defence.

Fig 36(a)   The back foot is taken well back so that you have more time to play the shot.

Fig 36(b)   A high front elbow helps the top hand with control.

Fig 36(c)   The bat face is angled forward to keep the ball down.

KEY POINT

For back defence:

1.   The further back you go the more time you have to play the ball.
2.   Angle the face of the bat forward to keep the ball down; there is no follow-through (see Fig 36(c)).
3.   Let your front foot come back naturally.

Forcing Shot

This shot is taken off the back foot and is played to a short-pitched ball which does not rise above stump height. It is very similar in technique to the back defensive shot, but is played for a different purpose.

1.   Although the feet movements are similar to those in the back defensive shot, the power is obtained by quickening the downswing and punching with the bottom hand just before impact.

Figs 37(a) and (b)   The forcing shot.

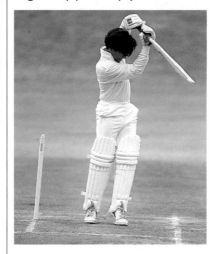

Fig 37(a)   A good position at the crease.

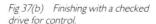

Fig 37(b)   Finishing with a checked drive for control.

2. To have really good control a checked finish is advisable (*see* Figs 37(a) and (b)).
3. A full follow-through, however, enables the ball to be hit harder and gives the batsman a lot of satisfaction.

Pull Stroke

Generally played to a short delivery below chest height, that is missing the stumps on the leg-side. As a batsman becomes more proficient, he might be able to pull balls from outside the off stump, though he will not be able to hit them past the square leg.

1. The back foot is moved back and outside the line of the ball, whilst the front foot is taken away to the leg-side to open up the body (*see* Fig 38(a)).
2. As the bat is brought down and across the body, your body-weight moves from the back foot to the front foot.

Hook

Played to a very short, fast, lifting ball, which if missed will pass over a right-handed batsman's left shoulder (*see* Fig 39).

The shot should only be played by very competent batsmen, in other words, those who can safely 'avoid' the ball when it is not in the right line for hooking.

1. Keep your eyes on the ball.
2. Because of the pace of the ball the body will pivot on the back foot.
3. The mechanics of the shot are similar to the pull stroke, but aim to hit the ball behind the square leg.

Fig 39 The hook – Dean Jones (Australia) showing a well-balanced, controlled finish.

Figs 38(a) and (b) The pull stroke.

Fig 38(a) A high backlift – the back foot has been taken back and across to open up the body.

Fig 38(b) The finish – body-weight has been transferred to end on the front foot with a good follow-through of the arms.

Figs 40(a)–(d)   The square cut.

Fig 40(a)   The start of a high backlift with good turning of the front shoulder.

Fig 40(b)   The ball has been hit down and all the weight is on the back leg.

Fig 40(c)   The completion, with the bat following through to a comfortable finish. Note that the bottom hand has climbed over the top one.

Square Cut

This is played to a widish, short delivery outside the off stump, and is a difficult shot to play on a pitch of uneven bounce.

1.   From a nice, high backlift the head and front shoulder are turned towards the line of the ball. A lot of the weight has already been transferred to the back foot (*see* Fig 40(a)).
2.   The ball is hit down so that it goes

> **STAR TIP**
>
> *Aim to hit the ball past cover's left hand. Against the pace bowler the ball will go behind square. With the medium pacer the ball will go squarer. Hit the ball down (see Fig 40(b)).*
>
> Peter Willey
> (Leicestershire and England)

Fig 40(d)   The batsman has hit the ball just in front of square.

behind square (*see* Fig 40(b)). Body-weight is now fully transferred as the ball is hit.
3.   The shot is completed with the bat following through comfortably to finish with the bottom hand climbing over the top one (*see* Fig 40(c)).

Leg Glance

Generally, this is a ball which is played to short of a length and aimed at the leg stump. In some respects it is played in a similar way to the back defensive shot.

1.   The batsman steps back – in Fig 41(a) good use of the crease is seen.
2.   At the point of contact the bat handle is kept forward of the blade of the bat (*see* Fig 41(b)).
3.   Allow the wrists to angle the bat and aim to hit the ball behind the square leg (*see* Fig 41(c)).

Figs 41(a)–(d)   The leg glance.

Fig 41(a)   Moving back on to the leg stump.

Fig 41(b)   The bat handle is in front of the blade of the bat.

Fig 41(c)   The ball is glanced behind square leg.

Fig 41(d)   A nicely balanced finish for a delicate shot.

4.   Keep your body well balanced throughout the shot (*see* Fig 41(d)).

Hitting Through Mid-Wicket

Generally played to an over-pitched ball on the leg stump, either with a half-pace forward to a full length, or from the crease to a ball of even fuller length.

1.   The upper body-weight is forward with the head leading to allow (as Graham Saville says in the Star Tip on this page), the ball to be played close to the body and late (*see* Fig 42(a)).
2.   A the moment of contact the bottom hand accelerates and closes the face of the bat (*see* Fig 42(b)).

Forward Play

This is generally regarded as easier than playing back, but there is, nevertheless, a sound technique required to play forward well, with great emphasis placed on the head position and leading front shoulder.

Forward Defence

Played to a good length ball on line with the wicket or just outside the off stump.

1.   A good lead with the head and front shoulder is required (*see* Figs 43(a) and (b)).
2.   Move the front foot as near to the pitch of the ball as possible and just inside the line of the ball.
3.   Bend the front knee to allow your body-weight to be transferred on to it, with your head positioned well forward and your eyes level (*see* Fig 43(c)).

Figs 42(a) and (b)   Hitting through mid-wicket.

Fig 42(a)   The head leads into the shot.

Fig 42(b)   Viv Richards whips the ball away and finishes nice and high.

Figs 43(a)–(d)   Forward defence.

Fig 43(a)   Keep the bat up, your head still and be ready to move forward.

Fig 43(b)   A good knee bend with your weight going forward is needed.

Fig 43(c)   With the bat angled, keep the ball down.

Fig 43(d)   There is no gap between the bat and pad.

Fig 44   *David Gower driving through mid-on against the Australians.*

4.   Extend the back leg with the outside of your big toe grounded.
5.   Angle the bat handle forward in front of the blade of the bat, keeping your top hand in control.

RULES CHECK

A batsman cannot be stumped off a no ball but he can be stumped off a wide ball.

Drives

Off, straight and on drives are some of the most satisfying shots a batsman can play. Properly executed, they limit the bowler's options as he becomes afraid to pitch the ball up too far.

Forward drives are played to a half-volley pitching from just outside the off stump to just outside the leg stump.

KEY POINT

During drives:

1.   Keep your head still throughout the shot.
2.   Use the checked drive against quicker bowlers as the speed of the ball just needs to be timed correctly.
3.   Use the full follow-through against spinners, particularly on slow outfields where more force is required to get the ball past fielders.
4.   Drop the front shoulder slightly and open the front foot a little during the on drive – this is more difficult than most.

1.   The head and front shoulder should lead the front foot so that it is just inside the line of the ball (*see* Fig 45(a)).
2.   Transfer your body-weight on to your bent front knee and make sure that contact between bat and ball is made close to the front foot.

RULES CHECK

Law 33   Handled the ball
1   Out handled the ball. Either batsman on appeal shall be out Handled the Ball if he wilfully touches the ball while in play with the hand not holding the bat unless he does so with the consent of the opposite side.

3.   Let your hands lead the follow-through in the intended direction of the shot.
4.   Lift your back heel but do not allow your back foot to pivot (*see* Fig 45(b)).
5.   For the checked drive keep your wrists locked (*see* Figs 45(c) and (d)); for the full follow-through allow your wrists to break and finish with your hands high (*see* Fig 45(e)).

STAR TIP

When driving look to hit straight with the full face of the bat. Aim between mid-off and mid-on a lot of the time.
Alan Lamb .
(Northamptonshire and England)

Figs 45 (a)–(f)
The forward drive

Fig 45(a)   *Leading with the head and front shoulder is the first essential.*

Fig 45(d)   *A checked finish seen from the front.*

Fig 45(b)   Half-way through the shot.

Fig 45(c)   A checked finish seen from the side.

Fig 45(e)   Hitting with a full follow-through can give a lot of satisfaction.

Fig 45(f)   An off-drive hit with power and precision.

Fig 46 Wayne Larkins
(Northamptonshire and England)
hitting a lofted drive 'on the up' and
finishing with high hands.

The Lofted Drive

Played to a full-length ball pitching on or
just outside the line of the stumps. Aim to
hit the ball into the open spaces over the
in-fielders, or whack it for six.

1. Hit the ball hard and keep the blade of
the bat on the path of the ball for as long as
possible.
2. Extend your arms and ensure a full
follow-through.

Moving Out to Drive

All the best players have good footwork –
it allows them to get the best positions for
playing strokes comfortably. Nowhere is
quick, correct footwork more necessary
than when moving out to drive. This
stroke is generally played against spinners
and to a well-flighted, good length ball.

1. After the first stride of the front foot
(see Fig 47(a)), move your back foot up to
a position just behind the front one – this
will ensure that your front shoulder is
leading down the line (see Fig 47(b)).
2. The front foot is once again led by the
head and the front shoulder as for a
normal drive (see Fig 47(c)).
3. Finish with a full follow-through for
maximum power (see Fig 47(d)).

KEY POINT

When moving out to drive:

1. Make sure that if you have misread
the flight and length of the ball you do
not get stumped. Be prepared to
defend or 'lay' something on the ball, for
example, the bat, a pad or a boot.
2. Do not set off down the pitch too
early as it gives the bowler a chance to
change his length.

Figs 47(a)–(d)   Moving out to drive.

Fig 47(a)   The first stride is made with the head kept still.

Fig 47(b)   The back foot is moved up behind the front foot and the eyes are level.

Fig 47(c)   The front foot is moved to the pitch of the ball.

Fig 47(d)   A full follow-through of the hands finishes off a powerful shot.

Figs 48(a)–(d)   The sweep.

Fig 48(a)   The front knee starts to bend and the hands come down from a high backlift.

Fig 48(b)   The ball is hit down.

Fig 48(c)   A good extension of the arms to finish with.

Fig 48(d)   A well-balanced finish to the shot from the bowler's point of view.

The Sweep

This stroke is played to a good length, slow to slow-medium ball pitching just outside the line of leg stump.

1. As for all forward strokes, lead with the head and front shoulder out to the line of the ball.
2. Allow the front knee to bend fully and the back leg to trail (*see* Fig 48(a)).

3. Hit the ball down and aim to hit it behind the square leg (*see* Figs 48(b) to (d)).

Leg Glance

This stroke is played as another alternative to the good length ball pitched just outside the batsman's pads.

1. The head and front shoulder lead with the front foot landing just inside the line of the ball – if you missed the ball it would hit your pads (*see* Fig 49(a)).

2. Keep the bat handle forward of the blade of the bat at the moment of contact and allow your wrists to direct the ball towards the square leg (*see* Figs 49(b) and (c)).

Useful Hints

1. Against a swinging or turning ball the batsman should generally look to play it with the swing or spin. For example, with an away-swing bowler bowling to a right-handed batsman, the ball will move to the off-side and so the batsman will play the ball to this side. To try and play the ball to the leg-side means that the batsman must hit across the line of the ball, thus increasing his chances of getting out. Obviously, the field is set with the majority of the fielders on the off-side. To score runs therefore the batsman will have to make sure that: he does not miss scoring

Figs 49(a)–(c)   Leg glance off the front foot.

Fig 49(a)   A nice lead to the ball.

Fig 49(b)   The ball is on its way. There is no sign of the head falling to the off-side.

Fig 49(c)   A well-balanced finish to a well-judged shot.

off a bad ball; he can open the blade of the bat just on impact to direct the ball into gaps in the field; he sometimes plays the ball softly and is prepared to run quickly to pick up singles.

2.   On flatter, quicker pitches it is possible to drive at balls which are not quite half-volley length, as long as you make sure you hit through the line of the ball.

3.   On pitches of uneven bounce batting becomes more of a lottery. Cutting and pulling are then quite risky shots and playing with a straight bat is even more essential.

4.   On slower pitches it is not so easy to play nice, flowing drives, even to balls which are slightly overpitched as the ball tends to 'stop' a little. A batsman would need a 'long' half-volley if he was to play a drive with confidence.

Possible Faults

Grip, Stance and Backlift

1.   Having your hands too far apart on the bat handle generally results in your bottom hand taking control, thereby causing problems in hitting straight bat shots correctly.

2.   If your top hand is too far behind the handle there is no chance of having a full follow-through.

3.   Standing with your feet too close together in the stance can cause poor balance; if your feet are too far apart it is difficult to have easy movement.

4.   If your eyes are not level to start with, there is the possibility that your head will fall to the off-side when you play a shot. A loss of balance might occur and control of direction will suffer too.

5.   Not picking the bat up straight can cause you to play across the line of the ball.

6.   Not picking the bat up until the ball is half-way down the pitch can result in a hurried stroke with poor control.

7.   Having a restricted backlift (not keeping the bat back and high) will mean a loss of power.

Fig 50   The batsman has turned on his back foot and has pushed through with his hands.

Fig 51   The left leg has not been brought back far enough and there is no chance of transferring the weight on to it.

Back Defence and Forcing Shot

1.   If you do not use the depth of the crease to good advantage (if you do not go back and across it enough with your back foot) you will lessen the amount of time you have to play the shot.

2.   If you do not keep your back foot parallel to the crease your body will not be sideways and, therefore, your bat could come across the line of the ball (see Fig 50).

3.   If your head leans away from the bowler, the balance of your body is affected and you could hit the ball into the air.

4.   Allowing your bottom hand grip to be too strong could result in the bat going across the line of the ball.

5.   If your front elbow is not kept high it will be difficult to play the ball down.

Pull Stroke

1.   By not taking your back foot backwards and to the off-side your head will not be in line with the ball.

2.   If you leave your front leg anchored you will find difficulties in getting at the ball and hitting it with control (see Fig 51).

3.   If you try to hit the ball too hard there is a danger that your head will turn away too early thus causing a mistimed shot.

4.   Restricting the backlift can lead to the ball being hit in the air – the bat should come down on the ball.

5.   Hitting the ball with cramped arms will mean a loss of power.

Hook

1.   If you move too slowly on to your back foot your arms may become too cramped.

2.   If you try to hook a ball which would not pass over your left shoulder if it was missed, you might edge the ball into your face.

3.   Do not play the shot out of bravado, when it would be wiser simply to take avoiding action.

Square Cut

1.   By not lifting the bat up high enough in the backlift, you may hit the ball into the air.

2.   If you do not move your back foot backwards and across you will have poor weight transfer and poor control of the stroke (see Fig 52).

Fig 52 *The back leg is rather straight and does not allow much weight to be put into the shot.*

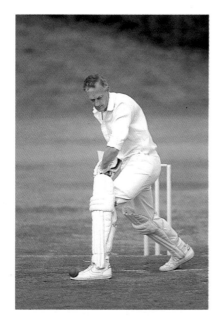

Fig 53 *There is no lead here with the head and front shoulder. The front foot has gone first and it is pointing down the wrong line.*

3. Playing the shot too close to your body restricts your arm movements.
4. If you do not allow your bottom hand to climb over the top one when completing the shot, the ball may be cut straight into the hands of the gulley or point.

Leg Glances

1. If you place your front foot too far inside the line of the ball, you will probably have to try to play around your front leg.
2. In attempting to glance the ball too finely you may give a catch to the wicket-keeper.
3. If you allow your head to fall to the off-side poor contact (if any) will be made.

Forward Defence

1. Moving your front foot first rather than leading with your head and front shoulder towards the line of the ball may cause problems in lining the ball up (*see* Fig 53).
2. If you only take a short pace with your front foot towards the pitch of the ball, you are likely to play the ball 'on the walk'.
3. If you play with a stiff front leg the stroke will not be played smoothly.
4. If you shut the face of the bat too early in the shot poor contact may be made and the ball might even be missed altogether.
5. If you play with rigid hands, instead of having your top hand in control and your bottom hand relaxed you may cause catches to be pushed to close in-fielders.

Forward Drives

The first four points given for forward defence (*see* above) also apply here, plus the following:

1. Coming up in the shot too early can lead to a loss of power as your body-weight is left on your back foot.
2. If you try to hit the ball too hard your head will often fall to the off-side resulting in a loss of direction (*see* Fig 54).
3. If you allow your bottom hand to come in to the shot too early, or if you allow your back foot to pivot, you may hit across the line of the ball.

Fig 54 *This head is falling to the off-side and this has resulted in the bat face closing and hitting the ball to the leg-side.*

Fig 55 *The back leg has collapsed and so all the weight has not been transferred to the front foot.*

4. A half-hearted effort to get to the pitch of the ball when moving out to drive will often leave you stranded.
5. If your back leg collapses your body will lean back thus making it difficult to keep the ball on the ground.

The Sweep

1. If you try to sweep an overpitched ball instead of a good length ball off line you will often miss the ball completely or mistime it.
2. If you hit the ball in the air, the bat was not hit down on the ball – possibly because of a poor backlift.
3. Turning your head too early (before contact is made) can also result in you missing the ball.

CHAPTER 7

FIELDING

The advent of one-day matches within the first-class game has dramatically improved the standard of fielding. Fielders chase hard, slide to hook the ball back from the boundary line, dive like goalkeepers to stop balls, and can often throw the ball 70m (70yd) into the wicket-keeper's gloves.

As in every other aspect of the game some players have an innate ability for fielding – they can pick up and throw well

even when they are off-balance. There is no reason, however, why all players cannot improve some quality of their fielding. It is not always possible to keep specialist fielders in their positions for all of the game and so there is a definite need for all-round fielders.

Catching

Close to the Wicket

1. Your weight should be evenly distributed between both your feet, and these should be about shoulder-width apart.
2. Your knees should be bent with your weight on the balls of the feet (*see* Fig 56).

Figs 56(a)–(c)   Catching close to the wicket.

Fig 56(a)   Your feet should be comfortably apart with the knees bent.

Fig 56(b)   Your palms should be facing the ball with your fingers pointing down.

Fig 56(c)   The ball has been caught well and some good concentration is shown.

3.   Your hands should be forward and together with your palms facing the ball and your fingers pointing down (*see* Fig 56(b)).

4.   Your hands should 'give' as the ball is taken (*see* Fig 56(c)).

Fielders who are at forward or backward short leg, silly mid-off and silly mid-on have to be fearless *and* sensible. They are there for the bat and pad catches, and not for the big hits, so they must be ready to take appropriate safety measures to avoid being injured.

Fig 57   David Gower takes a magnificent catch close to the wicket against the Australians.

High Catch

1.   Sight the ball and then move into the line of the ball quickly.

2.   If possible establish a base and try to catch the ball in front of your eyes.

3.   Keep your fingers wide and again let the palm of your hand and the front of your fingers face the ball (*see* Fig 58(a)).

This applies even if the ball is caught 'baseball' fashion (*see* Fig 58(b)).

Fig 58(a)   The fingers should be wide apart with the palms and the front of the fingers facing the ball in the high catch.

Fig 58(b)   An alternative method for the high catch – a 'baseball' fashion.

Fig 59   A first-class example of a close catch on the leg-side.

KEY POINT

When you are catching a high ball, do not point your fingertips at the ball as if you mistime the catch and the ball hits a fingertip you could be out of the game for several weeks.

Flat Catching (Skimmers)

Fielders at mid-off, mid-on, cover and mid-wicket often have the ball driven at them at about head-height.

Fig 60   The flat catch. As the ball is caught the head moves safely to one side.

1.   Keep the palms of your hands cupped in an inverted position, in other words, with your fingers pointing upwards.
2.   If the ball is coming directly at the face, move your face to one side as you take the ball into your hands (*see* Fig 60).

Ground Fielding

Defensive Interception

This is also known as the long barrier.

1.   Your right foot is at right angles to the line of the ball.
2.   Make sure that your left knee is in front of your right heel and 'watch' the ball into your hands by keeping your head over the line of the ball (*see* Fig 61(a)).
3.   Move your left foot forward ready for a return to the stumps (*see* Fig 61(b)).
4.   Finish with a determined follow-through of your throwing arm (*see* Fig 61(c)).

Figs 61(a)–(c) Defensive interception.

Fig 61(a) The left knee is positioned in front of the right foot and the ball is watched safely into the hands.

Fig 61(b) The left foot is moved forward ready for the throw.

Fig 61(c) The throwing arm has gone through towards the target.

Figs 62(a)–(d)   Attack interception.

Fig 62(a)   Going down to meet the ball.

Fig 62(b)   The ball is picked up just outside the right foot.

Attack Interception

This is one-handed interception and is used when the ball has not travelled far from the stumps.

1.   Move quickly and face the line of the ball (see Fig 62(a)).
2.   Pick the ball up just outside your right foot (see Fig 62(b)).
3.   Release the ball underhand as quickly as possible (see Figs 62 (c) and (d)).

KEY POINT

In attack interception it is the early release of the ball that runs batsmen out.

Figs 63(a)–(d)   Two-handed interception.

Fig 63(a)   A clean pick-up in front of the leading foot, with the left foot trailing behind.

Fig 63(b)   The trailing foot has been brought forward to get into a sideways position.

Fig 62(c)   A quick release of the ball . . .

Fig 62(d)   . . . can obtain a run-out.

Two-Handed Interception

Over a longer distance a fielder is better advised to use the two-handed pick-up.

1.   Move quickly on to the line of the ball.
2.   If possible turn your right foot square to the line of the ball and pick the ball up in front of your foot with both hands (*see* Fig 63(a)).
3.   Keep your left foot trailing behind to help with power when throwing.
4.   Point your non-throwing arm in the direction of the throw and throw at shoulder level (*see* Figs 63(b) to (d)).

Fig 63(c)The non-throwing arm can act as a guide to the target.

Fig 63(d)   A positive finish with the weight coming through to assist a powerful throw.

Retrieving

This is another form of attack fielding, although this time the ball has to be chased after.

1.   For middle distances it is generally best to pick up the ball on the outside of your right foot (*see* Fig 64(a)).
2.   If the ball is travelling fairly quickly, the fielder's momentum might mean that he has to take an extra stride or two after picking up the ball.
3.   A strong pivot (*see* Fig 64(b)) is required to get into a good throwing position.
4.   A flat throw (*see* Fig 64(c)), ending with a full follow-through of the throwing arm (*see* Fig 64(d)) can return the ball quickly and accurately.

When the ball is slowing down somewhere near the boundary and a long throw is required:

1.   Pick up the ball on the inside of your left foot (*see* Fig 65(a)).
2.   Give a vigorous thrust with your left foot (*see* Fig 65(b)) to help your body step towards the target (*see* Fig 65(c)).
3.   Move your right foot into position at right angles to the throwing line (*see* Fig 65(d)).
4.   A strong throw, possibly at forty-five degrees, completes the movement (*see* Figs 65(e) and (f)).

Figs 64(a)–(d)   Retrieving – middle distance.

Fig 64(a)   The ball is picked up on the outside of the right foot.

Fig 64(b)   A quick turn . . .

Fig 64(c) . . . and throw . . .

Fig 64(d) . . . puts the batsman under pressure.

Figs 65(a)–(f) Retrieving – long distance.

Fig 65(a) *Adjust your strides to pick up the ball.*

Fig 65(b) *Pick the ball up on the inside of the left foot.*

Fig 65(c) *The left leg thrusts the body towards the target.*

Fig 65(d) *The right foot is now at right angles to the line of the throw.*

Fig 65(e) *A vigorous follow-through . . .*

Fig 65(f) *. . . completes the throw.*

Figs 66(a)–(c)   Throwing on the turn.

Fig 66(a)   The ball will be picked up on the outside of the right foot . . .

Fig 66(b)   . . . followed by a jump turn off the left foot . . .

Fig 66(c)   . . . and a throw whilst still in the air.

Figs 67(a) and (b)   Throwing – general technique.

Fig 67(a)   All systems ready to go with the throwing arm bent and with a cocked wrist.

Fig 67(b)   A forceful follow-through with the head looking over the throwing shoulder.

Throwing

This tends to be one of the neglected skills on practice nights. Requirements needed for good throwing are: flexibility; strength; speed; and accuracy.

General Technique

1.   Pick up the ball with your right foot at right angles to the intended direction. Your weight should be on this foot and your knee bent.

RULES CHECK

Overthrows
Batsmen and fielders are often confused as to how many runs have to be counted as a result of overthrows. They need to refer to Law 19(5).

2. Let your front foot go towards the target. Your throwing arm, with your elbow bent and your wrist cocked is taken back from your shoulder (*see* Fig 67(a)).
3. Point your front arm in the direction of the intended throw and keep your head still.
4. Transfer your weight on to your front leg which you straighten and twist so that your body is pushed at the target.
5. Your body is then in a position to finish with a vigorous follow-through with your head looking at the target over your throwing shoulder (*see* Fig 67(b)).

Wicket-Keeping

'Goalkeepers and wicket-keepers need to be a little mad.' True or false? Well, it certainly helps.

There are a number of batsmen and bowlers in a team but there is only one wicket-keeper, and because of the nature of his job it might be as well to identify some of the qualities necessary for wicket-keeping. These are: bravery; determination; a sense of humour; enthusiasm; agility; concentration; optimism; stamina; and the ability to catch.

Stance

The wicket-keeper's stance needs to be comfortable and without strain. An ideal squatting position which keeps muscular strain to a minimum has:

Fig 68(a)   The wicket-keeping stance. It is important to be comfortable and well balanced with your eyes level. The back of your hands should rest lightly on the ground.

Fig 68(b)   A good clear sight of the ball is necessary wicket-keeping. Note the position of this wicket-keeper's left foot.

1. The seat close to the ground.
2. The weight equally distributed on the balls of the feet.
3. The back of the hands resting lightly on the ground.
4. The eyes level and chin up.

Standing Up

It is imperative that the wicket-keeper can see easily every ball being bowled. This generally means that his inside foot will be in line with off/middle-off stump and only about half a pace back from the stumps. If the batsman is large and fat the keeper may have to stand a little wider.

Standing Back

Again, the wicket-keeper should have a clear view of the ball. He may have to stand a little wider for a left-handed, over-the-wicket bowler. There is a danger in standing too wide, however, in that he cannot get across to a ball which is bowled down the leg-side. It is critical too, that the wicket-keeper establishes quickly how far back to stand. Obviously the pace of the bowler has to be assessed, so that the wicket-keeper can take the ball between knee- and waist-height.

Fig 69(a)   Although the ball has been hit, the wicket-keeper has assumed that the batsman will miss.

Fig 69(b)   As he takes the ball, the wicket-keeper's weight is on the foot nearest the stumps.

Fig 69(c)   The wicket-keeper has taken up a good position for an attempted run-out.

Fig 69(d)   By raising his hand above his head the wicket-keeper lets the fielder know where to aim for.

Wicket-Keeping Tips

1.   Assume that every ball bowled will reach you.

2.   Do not move into the stance position too early – it might mean too much stress for too long.

3.   Move only after the ball has been sighted and come up as the ball bounces.

4.   As you catch the ball let your arms become 'long' to allow for bending of your elbows and let your hands 'give'.

5.   Try to keep your weight on the foot nearest to the stumps when taking the ball.

6.   When taking returns from the field: try to be in striking distance of the stumps for attempted run-outs; clap your hands, or raise a hand above your head to let the fielder know where his target is; try to make poor returns look better by always catching the ball.

Figs 70(a)–(c) Stumping on the off-side.

Fig 70(a) Move the right foot to the line of the ball.

Fig 70(b) Keeping your weight on the inside foot and having fast hands help to make a quick stumping.

Fig 70(c) A good body turn helps to take a sudden lifting ball.

Fig 71 A brilliant catch on the off-side.

Stumping

On the off-side:

1. Move your right foot to the line of the ball (*see* Fig 70(a)).
2. To help in breaking the wicket speedily, keep your weight on your inside foot (*see* Fig 70(b)).
3. Be prepared to move off the line if the ball lifts suddenly (*see* Fig 70(c)).

On the leg-side:

1. Move your left foot once the line is judged (*see* Fig 72(a)). If the ball is quite wide, extra foot movements will be required (*see* Fig 72(b)).
2. Keep your weight on your inside foot.
3. Keep level as you move.
4. As when taking on the off-side a fast hand action is a big asset (*see* Fig 72(c)).

Keep fit and lively.

Figs 72(a)–(d)   Stumping on the leg-side.

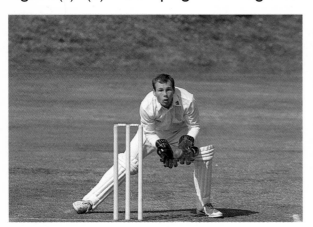

Fig 72(a)   The first requirement is to move your left foot to the line of the ball.

Fig 72(b)   Extra foot movements are necessary for this wide leg-side delivery.

Fig 72(c)   A fast hand action gives the wicket-keeper a chance of a stumping.

Fig 72(d)   This lifting ball is well taken.

Useful Hints

1.   Close catching – fielders need to have good, quick reflexes and above all 'safe' hands. Slip fielders have to be able to dive and it is a big advantage to be able to catch with either hand. As well as being able to move quickly, the bat/pad specialists have also to be brave, as a good hit off a bad ball could prove very dangerous.

2.   Fielders on the boundary – the third man and fine leg should be good ground

Bruce French dives to stop the ball from going to the boundary.

Catching Away from the Wicket

1.   Setting off too quickly and early without appreciating the pace and line of the ball can lead to a missed catch.
2.   *See* Point 4 above.
3.   If you do not keep your hands and arms relaxed the ball might bounce out of your fingers.
4.   Being off balance makes it difficult to catch the ball.

Ground Fielding

1.   Not bending down sufficiently allows the ball to go underneath your hands.
2.   Not releasing the ball as soon as possible after fielding it gives the batsman more time to reach the crease safely.
3.   Leaving your body-weight on your back foot when throwing can mean a lack of distance and power in the throw.

fielders and have strong arms. By being good throwers, if the ball comes straight to them they will be able to prevent the batsman from taking more than one run. The other fielders on the boundary, who are generally there for the spin bowlers, should ideally be fleet of foot, have safe hands and be able to return the ball quickly to the stumps. The 'sweeper' on the off-side boundary (often there when a run chase is on) is another fielder who has to attack the ball and return it swiftly to prevent a second run being taken.
3.   For those who have to be in the mid-field, the ability to move quickly, pick the ball up cleanly and return accurately is essential if they are to pressurize the batsmen into making an error of judgement and prevent constant singles being taken.

Possible Faults
Catching Close to the Wicket

1.   Standing with the feet too wide apart makes it difficult to move quickly.
2.   Standing too close to the batsman means there is very little time to respond to the shot.
3.   If you are standing too deep, the ball might be dropping short.
4.   Attempting a catch with your fingertips pointing at the ball might mean a broken finger.

Wicket-Keeping

1.   By standing in 'no man's land', in other words, neither up to the stumps nor back far enough, the wicket-keeper will have difficulty in stumping and catching.
2.   Moving too early, before assessing the right line leads to poor handling of the ball.
3.   Watching the bat instead of the ball often means you miss the ball altogether.
4.   Getting into position too early causes your legs and back to become tired too soon in the match.
5.   Snatching at the ball instead of allowing the ball to come to the gloves may result in misses.

CHAPTER 8

SKILL-SPECIFIC PRACTICES

'Practice makes perfect' is an old saying that has an element of truth in it, however, a former colleague of mine always added 'if the practice *is* perfect'.

It is no good practising without purpose. Sometimes people practise just for the sake of it, but unfortunately, without proper supervision they end up practising faults. I have seen an expensive bowling machine being used by a batsman whose basic technique could not cope with the deliveries served to him. It was a waste of money and time, and he would have been much better off in a coached group type of practice.

On a club practice night with only one net available it is often very difficult to fit in a session which enables an individual to gain specific practice. However, if any difficulties can be surmounted, then a short concentrated period can be of great value to any cricketer who wishes to become a better player.

Batting Practices

1.   If a batsman is not driving the ball very well some practice with a dropped tennis ball could provide a start to his training (*see* Fig 73(a)).
2.   The batsman can then progress to driving a ball thrown underhand. The ball should be hit in the direction of the fielders (*see* Fig 73(b)).
3.   The batsman can now be padded up for a net session. The ball can be served by a bowling machine, if available (*see* Fig 73(d)), or by a thrower with the ball pitching on a half-volley length.
4.   A net session with bowlers who can bowl accurately would also help. It could be argued that one should not encourage bowlers to bowl half-volleys, but any bowler would bowl one if he felt it would take a wicket.
5.   If a few players needed driving practice a practice could be evolved which would incorporate the following: driving; running between the wickets; fielding; and wicket-keeping (*see* Fig 73(c)).

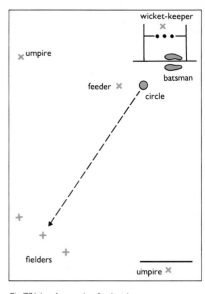

Fig 73(a)   Driving practice 1. The ball is dropped by the feeder from the batsman's eye level into the circle. The batsman drives the ball on the second bounce (half-volley) towards the fielders.

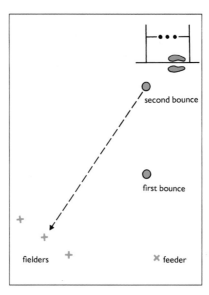

Fig 73(b)   Driving practice 2. The ball is served underarm and the batsman drives it on the second bounce. This is called a 'bobble' serve.

Fig 73(c)   A practice for batting, running between the wickets, fielding and wicket-keeping. The feeder serves the ball into the circle and the batsman drives and runs to the line and back. The fielders intercept the ball and return it to the wicket-keeper. If practised outdoors, the ball can be served underarm from the line – approximately 10m (10yd).

Fig 73(d)   England cricketers gain specialist practice using the bowling machine.

Batting practices for other weaknesses could be made along similar lines.

Bowling Practices

When a bowler is off form or wishes to practise new skills it is often best done, at least initially, in a net without a batsman being present. In these circumstances the batsman is a distraction as the bowler needs to be able to concentrate on learning or relearning a specific skill.

1.   If the bowler can obtain six to twelve good practice balls (difficult at many clubs) he should spend an hour in the net, preferably under supervision, until the skill is mastered to a reasonable degree.

2.   A wicket-keeper can then be introduced into the practice to help the bowler with his line.

3.   Finally, a batsman should come into the net.

This form of progression enables confidence to be developed and retained.

If accuracy is required a target area could be marked out with string, paper, tin-sheets, painted lines or with handkerchiefs (*see* Fig 74(a)). Again, practise without a batsman to start with – a wicket-keeper is very useful indeed though. Have a large target initially – 3 × 1m (3 × 1yd), for example – and then gradually reduce the size.

A further accuracy practice is to have the bowler bowling from a set of stumps to a single stump at the batting end. A further stump is placed about 4m (4yd) in front of the batting end stump, but in line with it and the middle stump at the bowler's end. Try to pitch the ball near to the target stump, but hit the single stump at the batting end (*see* Fig 74(b)).

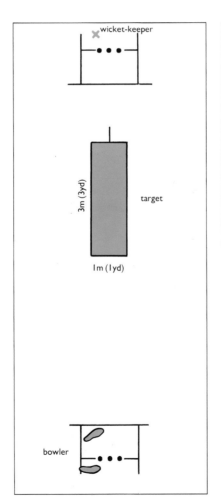

Fig 74(a)   A simple layout for bowling practice.

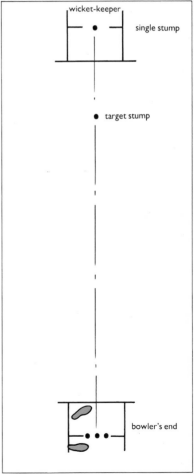

Fig 74(b)   A harder practice for bowlers.

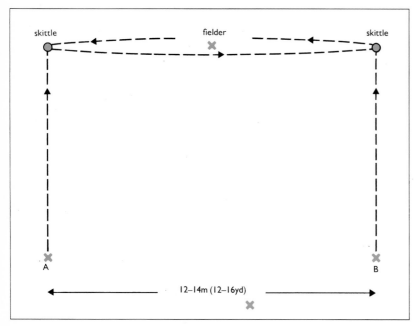

Fig 75(a) Feeder A rolls the ball to the skittle in front of him, and the fielder runs to intercept and return the ball. Feeder B then throws the ball in the air towards the skittle, and the fielder runs across, catches and returns the ball. This action continues non-stop for 30 seconds.

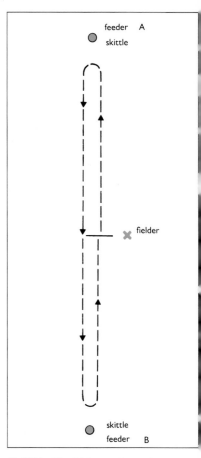

Fig 75(b) The fielder runs forward to intercept a ball from feeder A, and then he turns to run and catch a ball from feeder B. The practice continues for 30 seconds when the players change places.

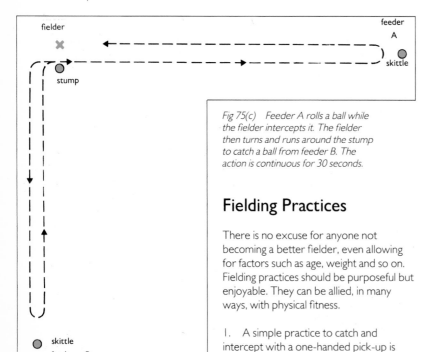

Fig 75(c) Feeder A rolls a ball while the fielder intercepts it. The fielder then turns and runs around the stump to catch a ball from feeder B. The action is continuous for 30 seconds.

Fielding Practices

There is no excuse for anyone not becoming a better fielder, even allowing for factors such as age, weight and so on. Fielding practices should be purposeful but enjoyable. They can be allied, in many ways, with physical fitness.

1. A simple practice to catch and intercept with a one-handed pick-up is illustrated in Fig 75(a).

2. A different organization as shown in Fig 75(b) can also be used for the same skills.
3. A third set-up as shown in Fig 75(c) can add variation to make these skill practices enjoyable.

Catching, such a vital element in our national game, needs to have its place in any practice session.

1. Catching off the bat for both short and long catches is easily organized (*see* Fig 76(a)). For short catches the fielders —including the wicket-keeper, who should

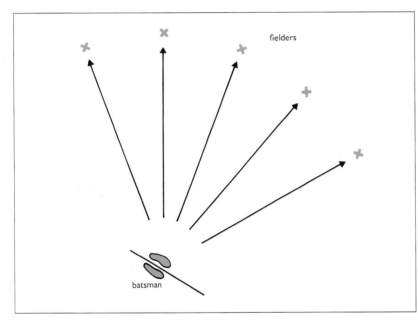

Fig 76(a)   Catching off the bat. The fielders throw the ball
underhand on the full toss. The distances between the
fielders and batsman may vary.

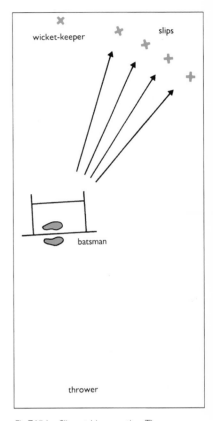

Fig 76(b)   Slip catching practice. The
ball is thrown at the batsman who
holds his bat at chest-height. The
batsman then edges the ball into the
slips cordon.

be wearing gloves – can be in an arc. For
longer catches the ball can be returned to
the wicket-keeper, who is near the
batsman who hits the catches. The wicket-
keeper should lob the ball so that the
hitter can find the fielders.
2.   A specific catching practice for slip
fielders is shown in Fig 76(b). Some
accurate throwing is necessary if this
practice is to be very worthwhile.

Wicket-Keeping Practices

Wicket-keepers who do not take the ball
cleanly down the leg-side on a good length
should practise without a batsman.

1.   Have the ball thrown on a good length
just outside the leg stump.
2.   Progress so that the ball is thrown to
land closer to the crease, until eventually
the ball lands nearly on the crease.
3.   Introduce a batsman and practise as
for 1 and 2, but have the batsman attempt
to 'nearly hit the ball'.

For catching practice on the move:

Fig 76(c)   A brilliant catch, showing the value of serious
practice.

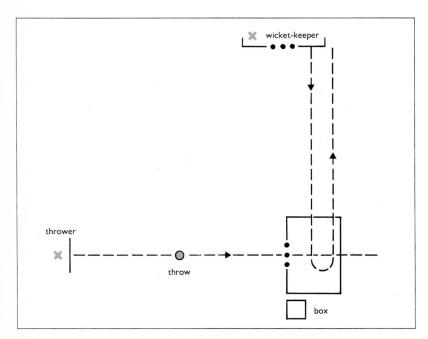

Fig 77 A catching and fitness practice for wicket-keepers. The ball is thrown as the wicket-keeper nears the marked-out area.

1. From a distance of 10m (10yd) and square of the wicket, run for six consecutive throws. After catching the ball in the marked area drop the ball into a box and return to your starting place to complete a circuit (*see* Fig 77).
2. Follow the instructions given for specialist training, Exercise 2(c), page 89.

Practice Methods

A sequence for learning and applying skills could be: group coaching; net coaching; 'middle' practice; games.

Group Coaching

Teaching cricket skills by group coaching methods is usually done when boys and girls are in the 10–14 age bracket. The method enables a class of twenty to thirty youngsters to be taught at once, and allied with the National Cricket Association Proficiency Award Scheme in England, it provides an excellent grounding for skill learning without undue pressure. Having

> **KIT CHECK**
>
> It is just as important to have the gear you use for practice, if it is different from your normal match gear, in good condition. On net practice night do not leave your gear lying about so that you do not lose it and so that others do not fall over it and damage it and themselves.

learned the basic skills during group coaching, they then have to be applied under pressure and where better than in the nets – providing that the practice is conducted correctly.

Net Coaching

Too often at clubs, net practice is regarded as more of a physical activity than an opportunity to have some meaningful skill application towards weekend cricket. There should really be someone in charge – the club coach preferably – to see that the evening's practice is disciplined,

purposeful, enjoyable and conducted in a safe manner. Nets can be quite hazardous if the proper safety precautions are not taken.

> **STAR TIP**
>
> *At its best net coaching and practice is probably the most effective, long-term method of improving batsmen and bowlers. At its worst it is the most overrated pastime, doing far more harm than good.*
>
> K V Andrew

Batsmen

In a normal net practice a batsman should have a set routine and generally play how he plays in a match situation. The format is usually as follows:

1. The batsman plays himself in, in other words, tries to find the pace of the pitch and what the bowler is trying to achieve. The sooner he can assess these problems the better.
2. Providing that there are not too many bowlers, one or two of them could be asked to bowl a particular line or length delivery which might have been troubling the batsman during matches.
3. Sometimes in a game a batsman may be required to defend when a quick number of wickets have fallen. Therefore, some practice in the nets at not getting out can be very useful.
4. Equally in a game he may be asked to get some runs quickly without taking too many chances or resorting to slogging. This too requires practice.

> **KIT CHECK**
>
> Whether or not to wear a helmet when batting is very much an individual matter. If, when facing quick bowlers, a batsman feels more confident with a helmet on, then he should wear one. Helmets are expensive for the individual but it may be possible for a club to provide one or two.

5.   Depending on facilities it might be possible to have a net against a particular bowler or a bowling machine so that a concentrated effort on a known weakness can be made without the distraction of other types of bowlers.
6.   A batsman may also keep getting out when nicely set during a match. A disciplined net practice may be of considerable use. A coach, captain or senior player could act as the other batsman and talk him through an imaginary innings until a 'target' of 25 to 30 runs has been achieved. Further chat could then help him to achieve another 'target'. By this means development of the batsman's concentration is helped.

Whatever type of net practice is available the batsman must practise with purpose. 'Practice often makes permanent' is another maxim, so if you practise the wrong thing continually it becomes part of your game and is often very difficult to eradicate.

Bowlers
Bowling in the nets has to be disciplined if any real satisfaction is to be gained. Too often when the nets are erected a single stump is stuck in at the bowler's end, instead of the creases being marked out and all three stumps put in place. These omissions can result in bowlers having problems with no balls when playing in matches. It often helps if you have an 'umpire' standing in.

To get the best out of his bowling practice the bowler should make sure that he is warmed up and ready to bowl as if

playing in a game. Types of net practice are as follows.

1.   If learning a new skill or relearning an old skill, bowling in an empty net under supervision can prove very beneficial – there is no distraction from having a batsman hitting the ball about. However, it will probably be very useful to have a wicket-keeper in this practice.
2.   A concentrated effort in a net to bowl a particular line and/or length to a batsman who has a known weakness is good practice. A lot of satisfaction can be gained when a plan such as this works.
3.   Often in a limited-overs match it is important to bowl a maiden over. It takes practice to achieve this skill. The bowler should attempt this practice with every different batsman he bowls to during the practice session.
4.   Inform the batsman as to the sort of field setting you would have if bowling to him in a match and then try to bowl to it in the net situation.

Wicket-Keepers
Because of the limitations of space available in a net there is no opportunity for a wicket-keeper to gain practice at standing back. However, there should be no problem in seeing that there is enough room behind the stumps for him to stand up to them. A quiet word with the groundsman should take care of this problem. Types of net practice for a wicket-keeper are given below.

1.   Practise with only bowlers so that the wicket-keeper can learn to 'read' what a bowler is trying to do with the ball.
2.   In the normal net with four to six bowlers a wicket-keeper can have a very busy time indeed. It is better for him to have fewer bowlers to keep to and preferably all of these should bowl at the same speed. The wicket-keeper should operate in short spells so that there is not too much strain on his legs and back. With six bowlers in a net he would be up and down like a yo-yo, would have little time to concentrate and would also be subject to considerable strain.

Middle Practice

The really skilful cricketer is one who can produce the skills in a match. The nearest substitute for an actual game is middle practice. This gives all who take part a chance to see their skills training put under pressure.

With a squad of about fourteen players it is possible to have: two batsmen; two batsmen padding up, or acting as umpires or scorers (if necessary); three seamers operating from one end; and three spinners operating from the other end. The batsmen can bat for twenty to thirty minutes, attempting to score as often as possible. The three seamers can bowl non-stop for about half of the batsmen's time and then the spinners can do the same.

Middle practice can help the players in the following ways.

1.   Batsmen can work out where they can score runs and can improve their running between the wickets.
2.   Bowlers can work out tactics to employ when a run chase is on.
3.   Fielders can field in pressure situations and will see that backing up pays dividends.
4.   Wicket-keepers can really get to know what bowlers are trying to do.
5.   Captain can sort out field settings and gain the opportunity to experiment with bowlers.

Fig 78(a) Backing up – fielders. The wicket-keeper is about to receive the ball. If he misses there are at least two fielders in line behind him who are nicely spaced to catch the ball.

The club coach should be there to give advice, direct proceedings, and see that the practice goes smoothly and that all have a worthwhile opportunity to test their skills under pressure.

Cricket Awareness

Middle practice is also a chance to appreciate cricket awareness, in other words, become alert to some of the fundamentals of the game. Players should be aware of the following points.

1. The non-striking batsman should be backing up (*see* Fig 78(b)). This will allow the first run to be made quickly or an early decision to be taken.
2. If only one fielder chases the ball to the boundary he might possibly need some help.
3. A batsman who drives every ball of an over to deep mid-off and never scores a

Fig 78(b) Backing up – batsman. The non-striker is backing up as the bowler is in his delivery stride. Note that the fielder is on the move too.

Terry Alderman at the completion of his follow through.

1. The striker should do the calling when the ball is hit in front of his wicket, and the non-striker should call when it is hit behind. There are 'grey' areas, for example, when the ball is hit just behind the square leg or point. Often the striker is in a better position to judge and, therefore, should make the call.
2. The calls to make are 'yes', 'no' or 'wait'. If 'wait' is called then it should be followed as quickly as possible by 'yes' or 'no'.
3. The sooner a call can be made the better it is.
4. The first run should be made quickly so that pressure is put on the fielder. The batsmen can pass comment as they cross, such as 'only one' or 'look for a second', or 'what about a third?'
5. The call for the second or third run is generally made by the batsman running towards the wicket which is likely to have the ball thrown at it.
6. A batsman must be ready to change the bat from one hand to another when running so that he can see the ball easily. This helps in making an early decision.
7. The non-striker should back up, in other words, walk quickly down the wicket for a couple of yards or so and be ready to run as soon as the ball has been bowled. However, he must make sure that his bat is kept behind the batting crease until the ball has been bowled.
8. When completing a run, batsmen should slide the bat in, or touch down over the crease when preparing for a second or subsequent run.

As with all of the other skills required for batting, running between the wickets should be practised. In the majority of schoolboy and junior matches too many wickets are lost by poor running between the wickets. Some attention can be given to the basics on practice night to help eliminate some of the mistakes that end up in the score-book as 'run out'.

run could obtain a single if given a little push.
4. Batsmen should make sure that they know which fielders throw left- or right-handed.

Running Between the Wickets

It was not until I saw a first-class county play that I really appreciated the value of good running between the wickets. In the match I saw, Derbyshire were playing and the openers were C. Elliott and A. Hamer (the former was later to become a Test match umpire). They seemed to have a certain understanding and to me, a young man, this bordered on the miraculous.

The chief principles for good running between the wickets include the following points.

PART 3
TACTICS

CHAPTER 9

CAPTAINCY AND TACTICS

Raymond Illingworth once said of captaincy, 'he needs the patience of a saint, the diplomacy of an ambassador, the compassion of a social worker and the skin of a rhinocerous.'

The captain does not necessarily have to be the best player in the side. Obviously it is to the team's advantage if he is a good player, but it is the ability to get the best out of his players that makes a good captain stand out. He needs to be alert and enthusiastic at all times during a game, giving thought to possible changes of bowling and fielding positions or, possible changes in the batting order when his side is batting. After writing down the batting order the captain should always put at the bottom 'sta' – subject to alteration!

It is clearly impossible to write about every cricket tactic for every sort of bowler against every different batsman. What I hope to do is to mention a number of possible actions that could be taken.

A Good Captain

As the person mainly responsible for team tactics is the captain, it would be as well to dwell on the make-up of a good captain. The following tribute from Dennis Lillee gives some indication of the qualities required for captaincy:

I have a healthy respect for the wonderful job that Mike Brearley did for England. From an opposing player's point of view it was obvious that his tactical manoeuvres were of an exceedingly high standard, a standard which he seemed to control and maintain with ease and with a maximum of team spirit. Being a highly intelligent guy, he obviously worked at the strengths and weaknesses of each individual under his charge and then marshalled his teams attacks and defences around them.

As a club professional for twenty-five years I can count the really good captains that I have played under on two fingers. I have respected a good number, however, because they were honest and were thinkers, even though I might not have agreed with their way of thinking. Respect from his players is therefore a high priority for a captain.

In club cricket the captain has to see that players enjoy their Saturday afternoon game. This generally means that each bowler gets a chance for a bit of bowling while each batsman gets a knock at the ball. It is not always possible, but the captain must be fair and weigh up the needs of the individual against those of the team.

The captain must believe in discipline, but generally he should remonstrate with his players in private. Bad behaviour or sportsmanship can often be dealt with there and then, on the field, and with great effectiveness.

A sound knowledge of tactics is also a necessity for any captain. He must:

1. Know the best positions for his individual fielders.
2. Know when to attack or defend and how best to do this.
3. Try to be positive at all times.
4. Know the players who like remorseless encouragement and those who respond to curses or being pushed.
5. Try to give sympathy and support when necessary, but be ready to pounce on slackness.
6. Set standards of punctuality, dress and behaviour on the field.
7. Talk to young players who come into the side.

The duties of a captain should include meeting the visiting captain when he arrives, and having a chat with the umpires on their arrival and not forgetting to thank them after the match, even if he feels that they have not umpired well. Umpires have the job of running the game and captains are responsible for helping them by seeing that decisions are accepted without dissent.

When his side is batting, the captain must make sure that his batsmen know what is required of them in terms of run rate and so on. When his side is fielding he has to get his bowlers and fielders working together, being careful not to overbowl his main bowlers.

Field Placing

One of the main jobs of the captain when his side is fielding is the setting of the field for his bowlers, generally done in consultation with the individual bowler. (Some examples of field settings are shown in Chapter 10 – *see* pages 78–80.)

The captain should have a general idea of how he will set his field as the players go out on to the field. Basically his fielders should be in a position to catch (*see* Fig 79), to save one run and to save four runs, so the right fielders who can do those jobs should be in the right places. The field should also be set with reference to how the bowler should bowl – in other words, with accuracy of line and length. It is no good setting the field for the bad ball.

A standard pattern is for a split 6–3 field, in other words, with six men on the side of the field to which the ball is likely to

Fig 79 Fielders in a position to catch, and what a catch it is!

be played. The captain must also be aware that if the ground is slow fielders should be close and squarer to the wicket, while if the outfield is fast and hard then the fielders should be deeper and finer.

There are factors, however, which may cause alteration to these tactics and the captain should be aware of them. These factors are:

1. The attitude of the batsman – is he defensive or attacking?
2. The condition of the ball.
3. The type of batsman – does he play straight or not?
4. The capability of the bowler – can he bowl an off-cutter, for example?
5. The state of the pitch.

In the final analysis the responsibility for field placing belongs to the captain. He must keep both his mind and his field settings flexible between attack and defence.

I like the story of the captain of a Minor Counties side in England who asked his very experienced opening bowler which end he wanted to bowl from. The bowler replied that he would bowl from the end with the dark brick wall behind him, adding

that the umpire at that end was also an old friend of his. He was right too – tactics or gamesmanship?

Pre-Season Tactics

The captain should look at what he envisages as his strongest side. Obviously there will be team changes which affect this but, by and large, the captain will know what the basis of the side will be. He can then decide whether his side is stronger in batting or bowling, is a good all-round side or whatever.

Winning the Toss

If a captain possesses a strong bowling side he will, in the majority of games, be inclined to put the opposition into bat if he wins the toss. He will hope, therefore, to bowl them out in a time-limited game or, in a limited-over match be at least good enough to restrict the total so that his side does not have too big a total to chase. To make the best use of his bowling strength he must attack, keeping his fielders in catching or attacking positions as long as he

can, and certainly trying to put pressure on new batsmen. He should only go on the defensive when absolutely necessary.

If a captain possesses a strong batting side he may be inclined to bat first if he wins the toss. He would then hope to pile on as many runs as possible in the hope of setting a huge target which would have a demoralizing effect on the other side. If he has to bat second his fielding tactics will hopefully be to take wickets, and at least contain the opposition so that his batsmen can attack any total they set.

On winning the toss the captain must also consider the following points.

1. The type of game, in other words is it a league match, a cup-tie friendly, an overs-limited match or a time-limited match?
2. The state of the pitch.
3. The strength of the opposition.
4. The weather.
5. The umpires – are they neutral or not?

Generally, in two-, three- or five-day games the pitch is at its best early in the game. Obviously the new ball has more bounce and is inclined to move off the seam or swing, but we all know this and the opening batsmen make due allowance for the fact. In a one-day game there is little change in the pitch over an afternoon if it has been reasonably prepared.

Knowledge of the grounds that you encounter must be a factor in making a decision on spinning up. If you know that a particular field dries out quickly and only causes batsmen problems for a short time then it may still be advantageous to bat first.

The length of the grass both on the pitch and on the outfield can also give food for thought. A hard pitch with grass which is not too short can be useful for seam bowlers. If the captain does not have any bowlers of this type, he may still decide to field first, particularly if his opponents have some good seam bowlers in their team. I was, however, taught as a youngster 'when in doubt – bat'.

Basically, every captain should have some plan of campaign but adaptability is

Fig 80   An attacking field for Australia versus England in 1989.

one of his requisites. It is absolutely great when the plan works, but whilst this may happen occasionally, most times the captain has to resort to some subtlety or other. For example, he might have to keep a good batsman back in case of emergency or promote No. 8 or No. 9 to slog a few runs quickly to get back into the game.

Other Tactics

The captain can also use the following tactics.

1.   On going out to field he should have his opening bowlers on at the right end. For example, an in-swing bowler would want wind blowing from the off-side to help him move the ball into a right-handed batsman, whilst an away-swing bowler would want wind blowing from the leg-side to help him swing the ball away from a right-handed batsman.

2.   The captain should ensure that his main bowlers (particularly the quickies) are not fielding where they have to chase the ball a lot.

3.   He should see that his specialist fielders are placed in their special positions, but he should also make them aware of the fact that they might have to go elsewhere.

4.   The captain should be close to the action and not hiding.

5.   He should attack as much as possible, even to the extent of risking losing the match.

6.   The game should flow even when the side is defending.

7.   The strengths and weaknesses of the opposition should be known to all, especially the bowlers. I remember in one important cup game that a local English club were drawn against a side from

Scotland. The home team won the toss and decided to bat. The opening batsmen played carefully against the opposition's opening attack and decided that if the bowlers were the opposition's best then they should get a big score against the rest of the attack. It turned out, however, that the Scottish side had kept their best bowler (Bob Massie of Australian fame) to come on as a change bowler and he promptly took wickets and changed the course of the game.

8. If a side batting first is out for a low score on a good pitch, there is little point in them trying to defend the score. It is better for them to go all out and attack with their fielders placed in catching positions in the hope that the opposing batsmen will feel pressurized into making mistakes.

9. It is always useful to have left-handed batsmen on the side. There are some bowlers who have great difficulty in bowling well if they are confronted by both a right-handed and a left-handed batsmen in together. The bowler has to change his line and his field placings constantly, and as a result will feel slightly frustrated and will lose concentration.

10. It is helpful if a batsman knows if a particular fast bowler loses his accuracy after bowling a certain number of overs. The batsman can then 'set out his stall' to defend well to start with and then look to score runs against the bowler later on.

11. Certain grounds have distinct slopes on them (Lord's, for example) and it is important that the bowlers who would benefit from such a slope are on at the right end. For example, it would be correct to have an off-spinner at the end where the slope of the pitch would assist his spin towards the batsman.

12. Sometimes a pitch is cut near to the end of the square. This makes for a 'short' boundary on one side of the pitch. It would generally be advisable to make sure that the spin bowlers bowl to the end where they expect hits to be made towards the longest boundary.

13. With so many cups and competitions available, a captain needs to know the rules and regulations of all of them. As they say in the Army, 'ignorance is no excuse'.

14. Making mistakes. The captain who has never made a mistake has yet to be born. To win or save a game a captain may have to try something unusual, for example, putting on an occasional leg spin bowler when it looks like the game is slipping away. As long as lessons are learned from mistakes made, players and spectators will accept them.

In limited-overs games, tactics will generally vary from a game which is time-limited.

1. If playing in an evening game, the captain who wins the toss should have no hesitation in batting first so that advantage can be taken of the best light.

2. With a limitation on the number of overs a bowler may bowl, it is quite often necessary not to let the main bowlers bowl their allotted span in one spell. It may be best to let them have six or seven overs out of ten to start with and then bring them back to finish off towards the end of the batting side's innings. Occasionally, however, if one of the bowlers is continually taking wickets in his first spell, it might pay dividends to let him complete his allotted number of overs in one go.

3. In a limited-overs match where it is known that one of the opposition's bowlers is really good, batsmen could concentrate on playing him very carefully and not being too bothered about the number of runs scored, while attempting to plunder the weaker bowlers.

CHAPTER 10

GENERAL AND SPECIALIST TACTICS

Playing an Innings

1. In the majority of times that a batsman goes to the crease his first thought should be of survival, allied with getting off the mark – in other words, scoring the first run. Trying to find the 'middle of the bat' is a phrase worth thinking about.

2. Once he has accomplished this first objective, his next objective should be to score ten runs. Having achieved this target his next aim should be to reach twenty, and so on. Having a definite aim, which is within the bounds of possibility, helps with concentration.

3. Talking with your batting partner is useful, as you can help each other to keep in mind what the objectives are, for example, how many overs there are to play for a draw, how many runs per over are required to win, or just to give advice on what a particular bowler's strengths and weaknesses are.

4. Once you have reached fifty runs, a century could be a possibility, but it might help to keep the target limited to ten runs at a time.

Fig 81   John Emburey bowling over the wicket at Lord's to Stephen Waugh.

Fig 82   John Emburey bowling around the wicket – what a difference in the angle of attack.

5.   It certainly helps if you know something about the bowlers before you start the innings. The more information you have in your cricket 'bank of knowledge', the better a player you will be.

6.   Getting into line against fast bowling is crucial and on a quick pitch take Michael Atherton's advice (*see* page 33). Against swing bowling generally look to play with the movement of the ball, in other words, an in-swinger should be played to the leg-side and an away-swinger to the off-side. Against the spinners it certainly helps if you are good at using your feet. If not, playing off your back foot might be the answer.

7.   Be aware of: the field settings for different bowlers; who the best fielders are and which of them are left-handed throwers; the batsmen in your side who are good judges of a run, and those who are slow runners between the wickets.

Tactics for the Fielding Team

Spin Bowling on a Good Pitch

1.   It is essential to bowl a good line – that line depends on the strengths of the individual batsman.

2.   With little turn from the pitch it is necessary to try more variations of speed and flight in the hope of making the batsman make a mistake.

3.   Using the width of the crease can be a successful ploy – if you do so it will give the batsman more to think about.

4.   All good spinners should have lots of patience and persistence in their repertoire. Do not let the batsman see any signs if you feel flustered.

5.   When bowling against aggressive batsmen who are scoring rather freely, make sure that the field is set correctly and that the fielders are in their best fielding positions. It is no good having someone with a 'poor' arm out in the deep.

6.   The 'floater' can be a real bonus if the spinner can manage to drag the batsman forward.

Spin Bowling on a Turning Pitch

1.   The off-spinner generally bowls around the wicket (an off-break from over the wicket would miss the stumps), pitching on the off-stump.

2.   If the pitch is a slow turner, it is probably best to bowl slightly quicker and with a slightly fuller length.

3.   It is policy to keep the batsman playing forward.

4.   If the ball is turning too much, keep calm and change your grip on the ball – the wedge grip will be suitable (*see* page 28, Fig 23).

Field Settings

The following show the positioning of fielders in various circumstances.

Field Setting A

The away-swing bowler (*see* Fig 83). When the bowler is quite hostile and the dictates of the game are favourable it could be advantageous to move the third man into the slip cordon. It is possible, too, that if the alternative ball to the away-swinger (off-cutter) is going well then the long, or fine, leg could be brought into a catching position. If the batsman is looking comfortable, the short square leg could drop back to a more orthodox square leg position to save one run and the second slip could move to re-inforce the covers. Fig 84 shows an attacking field with three slips, a gulley, a short leg and a silly mid-off. With the wicket-keeper and bowler in view this only leaves three other fielders away from the wicket. Another variation is to bring the third man up as a second gulley.

Field Setting B

The in-swing bowler (*see* Fig 85). If the bowler is really attacking and bowling a good line he will want to do without a third man. As the ball loses its shine and swings less the 3/6 field often becomes a 4/5 field with one of the short legs coming across either into the covers or going to third man. The other short leg can then go to normal square leg. Again after the initial burst, the backward short leg will probably go back to long, or fine, leg to save the four.

Field Setting C

The off-spin bowler on a turning pitch (*see* Fig 86). When attacking, a silly point is necessary for the bat and pad catch and two close-in fielders on the leg-side for catching are also needed. The short mid-on and mid-wicket can close any gaps and keep the pressure on the batsman. The deep mid-on and mid-wicket can at times be in position only three-quarters of the way back to the boundary for big drives that are mishit. The deep square leg is nearly always required for the sweep shot.

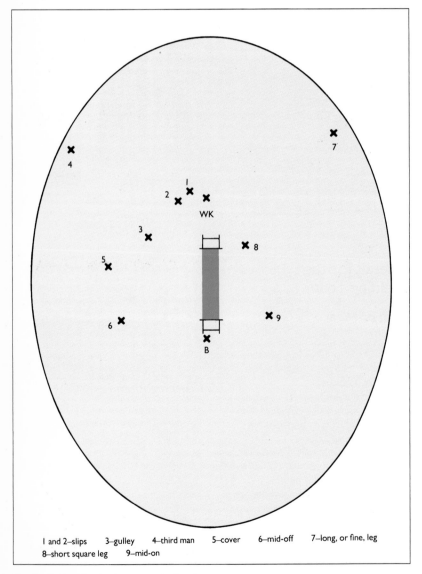

I and 2—slips   3—gulley   4—third man   5—cover   6—mid-off   7—long, or fine, leg
8—short square leg   9—mid-on

Fig 83   Field setting A – the away-swing bowler.

Fig 84　An attacking field for Geoff Lawson.

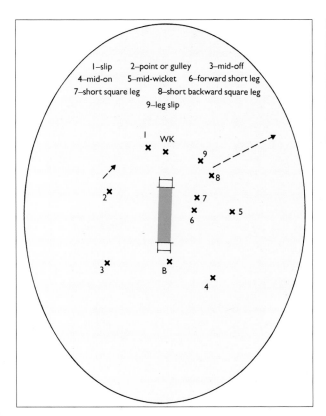

1—slip　　2—point or gulley　　3—mid-off
4—mid-on　　5—mid-wicket　　6—forward short leg
7—short square leg　　8—short backward square leg
9—leg slip

Fig 85　Field setting B – the in-swing bowler.

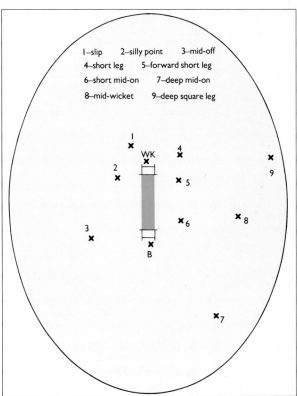

1—slip　　2—silly point　　3—mid-off
4—short leg　　5—forward short leg
6—short mid-on　　7—deep mid-on
8—mid-wicket　　9—deep square leg

Fig 86　Field setting C – the off-spin bowler and turning pitch.

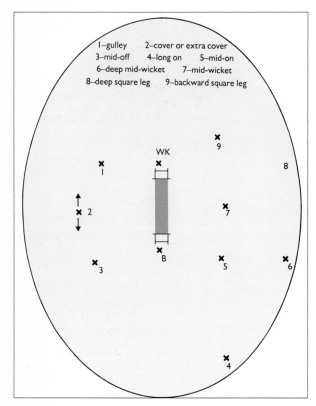

Fig 87   Field setting D – the off-spin bowler and true pitch.

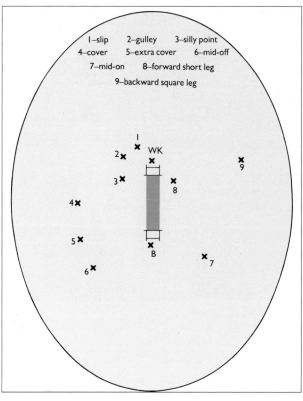

Fig 88   Field setting E – the slow left-arm and leg-spinner on a turning pitch.

Field Setting D

The off-spin bowler on a true pitch (*see* Fig 87). On a good pitch when the batsmen are attacking, the off-spinner will need to beat the batsman in the air rather than off the pitch. For this particular field setting the bowler will need to bowl a middle and leg line. Deep square leg, deep mid-wicket and long-on are back on the boundary, while backward square, mid-wicket and mid-on are all trying to save one run, as are the fielders on the off-side.

Field Setting E

The slow left-arm and leg-spin bowler on a turning pitch (*see* Fig 88). With the bowler bowling a middle and off line, he is hoping to have the batsmen playing mainly to the off-side. Four fielders, slip, gulley, silly point and short leg are all in close catching positions, with the rest all saving one run. If the leg-spinner bowls a googly which is easily spotted by the batsmen, a fielder might be taken from the off and transferred to the leg-side.

Field Setting F

The slow left-arm and leg-spin bowler on a true pitch (*see* Fig 89). Again the line is middle and off to off stump. The short third man is positioned to save one run. The deep cover is necessary if there is no turn at all as any ball fractionally short or wide will be worked square.

In first-class cricket the slow, left-arm bowler is often asked to try to contain batsmen by bowling on a leg and middle line and, therefore, a different field setting than the one shown would be required. The leg-spinner is not generally regarded as a containing bowler.

Field Settings – Conclusion

All the field setting in the world counts for nothing if a batsman comes into bat and proceeds to lambast the ball all over the park, or gets inside edges which scoot off to the boundary. At best, field setting can be a precise art, at worst a nightmare – hopefully the latter does not occur too often. However, if a batsman does bat in an unorthodox fashion, but is successful, it might be necessary to set an unorthodox field to get him out.

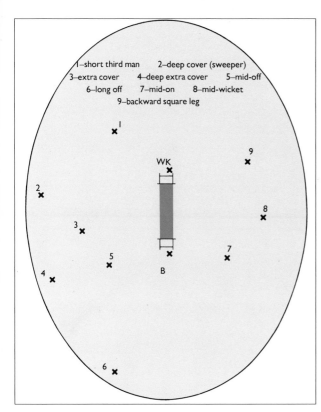

1—short third man   2—deep cover (sweeper)
3—extra cover   4—deep extra cover   5—mid-off
6—long off   7—mid-on   8—mid-wicket
9—backward square leg

Fig 89   Field setting F — the slow left-arm and leg-spinner on a true pitch.

Tactics for the Batting Team

Off-Spin Bowling

Right-Handed Batsman on a Turning Pitch

1. Basically, forget the off-side – especially wide of mid-off.
2. Stand still and let the ball come up. *Do not* push out hard at the ball.
3. Make sure that your back leg is covering the off stump.
4. Possible scoring shots are: hitting the overpitched ball between mid-off and mid-on; 'working' the ball on the leg-side; sweeping the good length ball which is off line.
5. Think aggressively and not defensively.

6. If going down the pitch, keep your head still and make sure that you 'lay' something on the ball – your bat, pad or foot, for example.

Left-Handed Batsman on a Turning Pitch

1. Stance is important – your back foot should be parallel and your front foot open.
2. If the bowler is coming around the wicket, close your stance up.
3. Play 'inside out' slightly.
4. Do not drive wide of mid-on; if possible drive through the bowler.
5. Hit the short ball square.
6. Aim to hit the overpitched ball over the top of extra cover.
7. If going down the pitch go towards mid-off and not down the line of the ball.

Problems Facing a Left-Handed Batsman

1. There are large numbers of in-swing bowlers who obviously bowl across left-handed batsmen. This increases the chances of slip and gulley catches.
2. The problem is the same as when facing off-spinners.
3. Try not to commit yourself to the shot too early when the ball is moving about.
4. Do not aim to force a full-length away-swinger ball wide of mid-on.
5. To counteract the away-swing bowler, particularly when he bowls from the edge of the crease, open your front foot out as this gives you a better view of the ball.

PART 4

FITNESS

CHAPTER 11

PHYSICAL FITNESS

Most club cricketers would agree that being fit is a good thing, however, persuading some of them to set aside time for fitness activities is another matter.

Practice nights generally give cricketers some batting and bowling practice, possibly with some fielding, but if a coach mentions that some fitness exercises will be part of the evening's activities, there will often be a limited response from the players. For those cricketers who earn their livelihood by doing heavy manual work there is an understandable reluctance to carry out further strenuous activities. However, if tackled in the right manner, with emphasis being placed on the fun element, most cricketers would come to accept that their performances could be augmented by improving their physical fitness. A number of players would also be willing to perform fitness routines in their own time, but it helps with team spirit if all the players take part as a unit.

Components of Physical Fitness

There are three main areas to consider:

Stamina – having increased stamina allows players to have a good work rate and keep a high standard of performance over a long period.

Strength – having increased strength can help bowlers to improve their speed, batsmen to hit the ball harder and fielders to run and throw quicker.

Mobility – being mobile allows you to twist, turn and perform the many actions required in cricket. Exercises can stretch muscles and provide protection against injury and allow the body to stay in good condition.

Fitness Training

Fitness training for all bowlers, batsmen and wicket-keepers generally follows a corresponding pattern, but there are variations caused by the different skills that each player needs to master.

Warming Up

Before taking part in any lengthy vigorous work-out it is most important that players should warm up. This prepares the muscles to do more strenuous work.

Some gentle jogging forwards, backwards and sideways, and running with very short steps with the knees raised high, followed by long loping strides will get the blood pumping around the body. This warm-up should then be followed by some general mobility work and stretching. See Fig 91(a) to (i) for some specific warm-up exercises. The warm-up period should take 10–12 minutes and will help reduce tension in the muscles, prevent injuries and prepare the body for more strenuous activity. Care *must* be taken to do the stretching slowly, avoiding 'bouncing' movements at the end of the stretch.

Fig 90   An essential part of a cricketer's day – warming up altogether.

Figs 91(a)–(i) Warm-up exercises.

Fig 91(a)   The neck. Stretch your neck to the right and left by dropping your head towards your shoulders.

Fig 91(b)   The shoulders. (i) Circle your arms backwards and forwards alternately. (ii) Together (come up on your toes when circling forwards), and (iii) 'cycle' with both arms pumping forwards.

Fig 91(c)   The hips. Place your feet shoulder-width apart and put your hands on your hips. Rotate your hips backwards and forwards in large circles. You can also place your feet at shoulder-width apart, and swing your arms at shoulder-height, sideways and backwards so that your eyes can always see your leading hand.

Fig 91(d)   The groin. With your feet astride, bend your right knee sidewards, keeping your other leg straight and your weight pressing inwards. Change legs.

Fig 91(e)   The back. Pull one leg towards your chest and keep the other as straight as possible. Try to keep the back of your head on the mat. Change legs.

Fig 91(f)   The quadriceps. Place your right hand on a partner's shoulder or against a wall. Take hold of your right foot with your left hand and pull your ankle towards your buttocks. Change legs.

Fig 91(g)   The hamstrings. Standing with both feet apart, turn your toes to face left or right. Bend your front knee keeping your back leg straight. Change legs.

Fig 91(h)   The calves. Put both your hands against a wall with your arms outstretched. Bend one knee and straighten the other to stretch the calf of that leg. Change legs.

Fig 91(i)   The ankles. Flex your ankles by performing a heel–toe action. Also, sit down, bend one knee and rotate your ankle by holding it with both hands. Change legs.

Figs 92(a)–(i)   Circuit training.

Fig 92(a)   Make sure that your arms straighten.

Fig 92(b)   Put your right leg on to the stool, put your left leg on to the stool, take your right leg off the stool, and then take your left leg off the stool.

Fig 92(c)   From a squat position thrust your legs backwards. Jump back into the squat position.

Fig 92(d)   From a prone position sit up until your hands touch your knees. Return to your start position.

Fig 92(e)   From a press-up position rotate your body in a circle using your arms and keeping your feet stationary.

Fig 92(f)   With your hands positioned behind your neck, lift your head and shoulders off the floor.

Fig 92(g)   With your feet resting on a stool, lift your hips using your hamstring muscles.

Fig 92(h)   With a brick or weight suspended from a stick on a piece of string, roll the stick until the brick or weight reaches it. Unroll the stick to return to the start position.

Fig 92(i)   With your hands resting behind you on a stool and with your arms bent, straighten your arms. Return to the starting position.

Circuit Training

What you do next depends on the amount of time and effort players are prepared to spend. Circuit training is for all-round conditioning and gives some emphasis on strength which can be very useful indeed.

A possible circuit could consist of:

1. Press-ups.
2. Step-ups.
3. Squat thrusts.
4. Sit-ups.
5. Arm circles.
6. Back raises.
7. Hip raises.
8. Wrist rolling.
9. Dips.

See Figs 92(a) to (i) for descriptions of these exercises.

Guide-Lines

1. Do two complete circuits.
2. Spend 30 seconds on each exercise.
3. Recovery time between exercises should be 30 seconds.
4. The number of circuits can be increased after a few weeks.

Note Expense is minimal as this set of exercises requires very little in the way of equipment.

Specialist Fitness Training

For those cricketers who have the time and motivation to be more involved with fitness, specific training for specialist aptitudes can be used.

Bowlers

1. Shuttle bowling – work as a pair in a net. One bowler runs in and bowls at the stumps and at the end of his follow-through he trots back to his mark. He repeats this five times. His partner, who has collected the balls then does his turn at shuttle bowling. Start by working for 15 minutes and then gradually increase the time span. It is important that attention is paid to maintaining good technique.

Figs 93(a)–(c) Strengthening work with a medicine ball.

Fig 93(a) Standing up.

Fig 93(b) Sitting down.

Fig 93(c) Lying down.

2. Some strengthening work in pairs using medicine ball (*see* Figs 93(a) to (c)).

(a) Standing up 1.8m (6ft) apart throw with a chest pass to each other, and then try a soccer throw. Gradually increase distance thrown.

(b) Sitting down carry out the same throws as above.

(c) One partner lies on his back while the other sits. Throw when you are lying on back and catch when you are sitting up.

Figs 94(a)–(c)   Weight training exercises.

Fig 94(a)   Bench press.

Fig 94(b)   Arm curls.

Fig 94(c)   Half-squats.

3.   Weight training (*see* Figs 94(a) to (c)) – an individual work programme should be worked out with an expert and done when properly supervised. Some simple weight training can be done without supervision.

(a) Bench press – lying on your back, push the weight (agreed by an expert) from your chest to the straight arm position. Perform ten repetitions.
(b) Arm curls – with your palms facing away from your body, hold the weight across your thighs. Lift the weight to your shoulders by bending your arms. Perform ten repetitions.
(c) Half-squats – hold the weight across your shoulders and behind your head. Half-squat and then straighten. Perform ten repetitions.

Batsmen
It is important that this training is done while players are wearing pads, batting gloves and carrying a bat.
   Shuttle running – in pairs and working alternately (*see* Fig 95).
(a) Sprint from the start line to line A – 18m (18yd). Touch behind the line with your bat. Each player works for 30 seconds initially.
(b) Variety can be introduced by each player sprinting to line C and back, to line B and back, and then to line A and back.

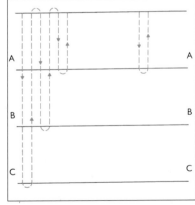

Fig 95   Shuttle running.

Figs 96(a)–(c)   Leg exercises.

Fig 96(a)   Squat jumps.

Fig 96(b)   Jumping on the spot.

Fig 96(c)   Squat thrusts.

Figs 97(a)–(c)   Shuttle runs.

Fig 97(a)

Fig 97(b)

Fig 97(c)

Wicket-keepers

It is important that this training is done while the players are wearing pads and wicket-keeping gloves.

1.   Leg exercises (see Figs 96(a) to (c)) – work for 30 seconds with a 30-second rest.
(a) Squat jumps.
(b) With your feet together, jump on the spot, bringing your knees to the chest.
(c) Squat thrusts.
2.   Shuttle runs – work in pairs

alternately (see Figs 97(a) to (c)).
(a) From a squat position behind the stump, run 5m (5yd) to the right around another stump, followed by a 5m (5yd) run to the left stump. Work for 1 minute.
(b) From a squat position 12m (12yd) behind a stump, run around the stump and back again to the squat position. Work for 30 seconds.
(c) From a squat position behind the stump, run 5m (5yd) to the left, dive on to a mat and attempt to catch a thrown

ball. Return to a squat. Work for 1 minute.

KIT CHECK

Keep your gloves in good repair, always making certain that the surface on the palms of the gloves is made of pimpled rubber. Keep the gloves pliable. Check them at the end of the season in particular to see if they need attention.

Figs 98(a)–(k) Stretching exercises.

Fig 98(a) Stretch for 20 seconds. (b) Stretch each arm for 12 seconds. (c) Stretch for 15 seconds. (d) Stretch for 15 seconds on each side. (e) Stretch each arm for 12 seconds. (f) Stretch each leg for 12 seconds. (g) Stretch each leg for 20 seconds. (h) Stretch each leg for 30 seconds. (i) Stretch each ankle for 25 seconds. (j) Stretch each leg for 20 seconds. (k) Stretch for 35 seconds.

Stretching

On a very personal level I have found over the years that the three most important aspects of fitness are warming up (including some stretching exercises), mobility work and stretching. The first two have been of the greatest benefit to me before and during a match and I have already discussed training for these. However, taking part in strenuous activity such as a cricket match or taking part in training on a practice night can make muscles tight and inflexible. My work with the Danish Cricket Association over the past few years has opened my eyes to the value of stretching. I have found it of particular value at the end of a match or a practice session – it helps to keep the muscles flexible and prevents a lot of stiffness on the following day.

How to Stretch

The correct way to stretch is with a relaxed and sustained manner, and with the mind concentrating on the muscles that are being stretched. The incorrect way is

Fig 98(l)–(u)   Stretching Exercises

(l)

(m)

(n)

(o)

(p)

(q)

(r)

(s)

(t)

(u)

Fig 98(l) Rock back 6 times. (m) Stretch each arm for 12 seconds. (n) Stretch for 20 seconds. (o) Stretch each side for 12 seconds. (p) Stretch each leg for 30 seconds. (q) Stretch for 3 × 5 seconds. (r) Stretch each side for 20 seconds. (s) Stretch for 20 seconds. (t) Stretch each leg for 20 seconds. (u) Stretch for 3 × 5 seconds.

to 'bounce' on the muscle. Easy, comfortable stretching reduces any tightness of the muscles. To start with spend only 10–30 seconds on an easy stretch, then as you progress, develop the stretch for about another 20 seconds.

Before following a stretching programme, note the following points:

1. There is a tendency to hold your breath when stretching. Avoid this as it means that you are not relaxed.
2. Your breathing pattern should be both slow and controlled.
3. After an easy stretch, slowly stretch a little further.
4. Always come out of a stretch slowly.
5. Do not overstretch.

The stretching exercises illustrated in Figs 98(a) to (u) have been very useful to me indeed. The arrow on the diagrams indicates where the effort is to be put in, while the shaded area shows the region where the stretch should be felt.

CHAPTER 12

COMMON INJURIES AND TREATMENTS

Common Injuries

1. Direct blows from the cricket ball to the head, ribs or thighs, arms and legs, feet and fingers.
2. Twisted ankles and knees.
3. Pulled muscles – hamstrings, groin, back muscles and so on.
4. Blisters.
5. Throwing an arm out or putting a finger joint out.
6. Grazes and scratches.

Treatment

1. With a direct blow to the head it is important to see whether the casualty is conscious or unconscious. Generally speaking a doctor or other specialist person is required to make a diagnosis and an early X-ray is necessary.
   Direct blows to muscles can be treated by placing an ice pack over the affected area and then applying some form of compression.
2. Twisted knees, ankles and minor sprains need ice treatment to control the swelling, as well as rest, compression and, if possible, some physiotherapy.
3. Pulled muscles need rest and then need to be strapped up. A pulled groin in particular needs rest and physiotherapy.
4. Blisters can be very troublesome and should be kept dry and allowed to heal themselves. Do not burst them with a pin or needle as this can cause poisoning. If you are prone to blisters it is possible to harden the skin beforehand by daubing the area with surgical spirit over a period of time.

5. If a finger joint is put out, it needs to be put back quickly, but by someone who is qualified to do so. The use of a finger stall might be helpful.
   Throwing an arm out can be very painful and needs professional treatment.
6. Many injuries sustained in the game are grazes and scratches. Though blood seeps out from all parts of a graze wound it soon stops of its own volition. Generally, you should clean the wound by rinsing it lightly with clean water and then gently dab the wound with a sterile pad until it is dry. If the blood is flowing freely, try to elevate the wound. When the wound is dry an adhesive dressing can be applied.
   For more serious bleeding injuries on a limb where there is no fracture, try to elevate the limb. Apply pressure with your fingers or with a bandage to stem the flow and then seek specialist medical aid.

Prevention

Some of the main causes of sporting injuries are:

1. Poor technique.
2. Overestimating one's ability.
3. Not being fit.
4. Poor warming up.
5. Inadequate footwear for the ground conditions.
6. Carelessness.

Sticking to sound techniques will ensure that your body is put in the right positions to cope with a hard, fast-moving ball – especially when catching – so that you will avoid a number of injuries.

As a batsman it is no good deciding to hook a fast bowler if you are not quick enough. It would be far better to take avoidance action and minimize the risk of being hit.

A lot of care should be taken in the selection of footwear. Cricket training indoors during the winter months is on the increase, but many sports halls have flooring which is not necessarily designed with cricket in mind. Cement, hard-grain wood blocks and so on, are not good for the legs even if the run-ups are covered with some form of matting. It is essential, therefore, to have footwear which will absorb a lot of the jarring which occurs both indoors and outside.

Adherence to the proper warming-up procedures, and attention to fitness levels of strength, mobility and endurance all have a part to play in avoiding pulls and strains. By wearing the proper safety equipment you will also avoid serious knocks.

Because cricketers are often very keen to resume playing, they often return to the game too quickly. After a muscle strain it is important to lengthen the muscle, in other words, it needs to be stretched. Repeated stress can lead to a rupture or more permanent damage. As someone who has had some plastic parts inserted in his knee, I know at first-hand how important it is to stick to an exercise programme and to complete it before attempting to make a quick return to action. Cricketers' knees and backs are prone to injury because of the nature of the game and so it is advisable to consult qualified physiotherapists who can give advice, not only on the treatment but on the rehabilitation as well.

CHAPTER 13

MENTAL TRAINING

Two words that I use a lot when I am coaching cricketers or managing a side are 'be positive'. Whether the circumstances of the game require you to attack or defend, or whether you are batting or in the field, there must be positive thoughts and actions to with the circumstances. A dictionary definition of positive is: 'absolute, unquestionable, definite, downright'.

Preparation for a Match

Self-Preparation

Ask yourself the following questions:

1. Am I fit?
2. Is my diet right?
3. Am I having plenty of sleep? (Sleep is the biggest producer of energy.)
4. Is my cricket gear in good condition?
5. Have I practised conscientiously?
6. Do I know the match rules?
7. Do I feel in good form? (Generally your body feels light when in good form.)

Some Positive Thoughts

1. I must have some recognizable ability or I would not be in the team or squad.
2. I am a member of a strong team or squad.
3. We are all good friends who have good team spirit and who help and encourage each other.
4. I have been well prepared and have practised hard.
5. I am capable of adapting to any environmental condition. The wind, the pitch, the run-ups, the outfield, the crowd, the opposition, the umpires make no difference. *I am in control of myself.*

If you can absorb these positive thoughts then your preparation is well under way.

Preparation when Batting

Physical Preparation Before the Game

1. Are any last minute looseners required?
2. Look at the pitch and the outfield. Make a mental note of the shape of the field.
3. In which direction is the wind blowing?
4. Have all your gear ready to put on.

Thoughts Before the Game

1. I will be as good as I can be.
2. I am opening the batting. Who will their opening bowlers be?
3. What do they do with the ball?
4. Where am I likely to score runs and where will it be difficult to score runs?
5. Is my opening partner a good judge of a run and is he quick between the wickets?
6. I will be as good as I can be.

It is no good for a batsman to say to himself before a game, 'Oh, I never make runs against this team, their opening bowler always gets me out'. To counteract this thought, he should try to think about the technique of the bowler rather than thinking of the bowler himself. One last positive thought could be: 'All I have to do is play one ball at a time'.

During the Game

I have already suggested earlier in the book a possible way to tackle playing an

STAR TIP

When batting it's a combination of things. If quick bowlers are bowling, I need to be determined as if fighting for my life. With spinners I'm more relaxed. Never try and hit the ball too hard. Remember, how you think affects how you play.

'Jack' Russell, *(Gloucestershire and England)*, on concentration.

innings (*see* pages 76 and 77). Positive thinking with the setting of 'gettable' targets will help.

After-Game Evaluation

Sit down after the game by yourself and analyse your innings – were you successful or not? Failures are wonderful opportunities for learning. Write down what was right and why; write down what was wrong and why; consult your coach.

Preparation when Bowling

Physical Preparation Before the Game

1. Are my bowling boots in good condition?
2. Have I got all my cricket gear organized?
3. Go and have a look at the pitch, and at the run-ups and the outfield in particular. Make a note of the wind direction and any slope that there may be.
4. Are any last minute looseners required?

Thoughts Before the Game

1. Which end would I prefer to bowl from? Why?
2. If I do not get that end I am quite capable of adapting to the wind, slope and so on. *I can cope easily.*
3. Basically my line will be . . .
4. My field placings are . . .
5. Their opening batsmen are . . . Where do they like to score runs? Their weaknesses are . . .
6. I feel good, I just need to have a nice rhythm as soon as possible.
7. I will be as good as I can be.

During the Game

1. Keep my mind on one aspect.
2. If the batsman is scoring runs in a particular area, is it because I am bowling the wrong line or length?
3. Would changing the field help?
4. Am I trying too many variations?
5. This batsman's hands are very high/low on the handle therefore . . .
6. A new batsman – I will try to pressurize him. How?
7. I am lacking in rhythm, I should concentrate on finishing the bowling action.

It is certainly no good thinking 'Their opening batsmen always make a century stand against us. There's not much point in bowling at them.' How can we get rid of negative thoughts like that? Again, by concentrating on technique. Make sure that the bowling action feels good – the emphasis is not to think about personalities but to keep concentrating on what is required.

After-Game Evaluation

1. Sit down by yourself to start with, and have a look at your bowling figures in the score-book. What do they tell you?
2. Runs were scored regularly in the . . . overs. Why was that? Were you thinking too much about taking wickets instead of concentrating on bowling well?
3. When did you bowl well? How did you feel?

4. Write down what was good.
5. Write down what was not so good.

As a result of this evaluation and after a chat with your coach you will be able to ascertain what you need to concentrate on. While learning concentrate on your technique and while competing concentrate away from personalities. When things have gone wrong it is often easy to analyse mistakes and learn from the situation. It is just as important to analyse when things go right as this will help you to gain a greater understanding of your game. Progress can be made from positive attitudes and efforts.

Preparation when Wicket-Keeping

Physical Preparation Before the Game

1. Have I got all of my gear – particularly my gloves and inners – in tip-top condition?
2. What about spares? Check on them.
3. Am I nice and loose or do I want to finish off with some stretching?

Thoughts Before the Game

1. I will be as good as I can be.
2. Who will be bowling first?
3. Go over in your mind what each bowler attempts to do.
4. Be quite clear about the spinners.
5. I must make sure that I keep the fielders on their toes, that I get to the stumps as soon as possible for returns and that first slip is in the right position.
6. I will be as good as I can be.

During the Game

1. Be prepared to give advice to the captain and bowlers.
2. Establish early on where you need to stand for each bowler.
3. Think about standing up to the medium pacers if you think it will put pressure on the batsman.
4. Do not move into the crouch position too early.

After-Game Evaluation

1. Sit down by yourself and ask yourself how you kept the wicket.
2. How many catches did I drop? Why? Did I move too early or too late, or was I snatching?
3. How many stumpings did I miss? Why? Did I have slow hands or was I snatching? Was I lacking in concentration?
4. If played well what was good – my concentration, level of relaxation or my foot movement?

Evaluation Form

Give yourself marks out of 10 for the following:

If you are honest with yourself, your answers could indicate areas in which you need to place greater emphasis.

Topic	Marks
Goal determination	(0 = none; 10 = completely determined)
Motivation	(0 = flat; 10 = charged up)
Worry	(0 = extremely; 10 = none at all)
Confidence in ability	(0 = none; 10 = complete)
Confidence in physical preparation	(0 = doubtful; 10 = complete)
Risk taking	(0 = not willing; 10 = willing)
Control of self	(0 = none; 10 = complete)

GLOSSARY

All-rounder   A player who is good at either bowling and batting, or at keeping a wicket and batting.

Backing up   When a fielder throws the ball at the stumps in an attempt to run a batsman out, another fielder positions himself some distance behind the stumps to prevent overthrows – this is called backing up.

Bagged a pair   Being out without scoring in both innings of a match in which each side has two innings.

Batting average   The number of runs scored by a batsman divided by the number of innings in which he was out.

Batting for a draw   The batting side is concentrating on not losing their wickets.

Bouncer   A bowling delivery slammed down hard enough on the pitch and far enough from the batsman's reach so as to fly at his head and chest.

Bowling analysis   The figures for a bowler's performance in an innings or series of innings. O = overs bowled; M = maiden overs; R = runs conceded; W = wickets taken.

Bowling crease   The line on which the stumps are pitched. The crease is 2.64m (8ft 8in) long and the stumps are placed in the centre of the crease.

Byes   Runs made off a ball which passes the batsman without touching his bat or his person.

Century   The name used when a batsman has scored 100 runs.

Duck   Being out without scoring any runs.

Full toss   A bowling delivery which does not touch the ground between the bowler and the batsman.

Going for the runs   The batting side is making a determined effort to score the runs necessary to win.

Good length ball   A ball which pitches in such a position that the batsman is not sure whether to play forward or back.

Googly   A ball which spins from the off-side to the leg-side, but which looks like a leg break.

Half-volley   A ball that pitches nearer to the batsman than a good length ball, thus enabling the batsman to play forward comfortably and hit the ball hard.

Hat trick   If a bowler captures three wickets in consecutive balls it is called a hat trick.

King pair   Out on the first ball without scoring in both innings of a two-innings match.

Leg byes   Runs made off a ball which touches a part of the batsman's body other than the hands.

Long hop   A ball which is short of a length and which can usually be hit easily.

Maiden over   An over from which no runs are scored.

Making an appeal   When the fielding side enquire of the umpire whether or not the batsman is out. The appeal is usually termed 'How's that?'

Playing back   This is the initial movement by the batsman which is made by moving the back foot towards the stumps. For example, back defence and attack, hook and pull.

Playing forward   This is the initial movement by the batsman which is made by moving the head, front shoulder and the front foot towards the pitch of the ball. For example, forward defence, drives and sweep.

Non-turf pitch   An artificial pitch – generally a mat of synthetic turf laid on a base of hard porous material or cement. The mat is pegged into the ground.

Over the wicket   When the bowler delivers the ball with his chest facing the stumps at the bowler's end.

Popping crease (batting crease)   This is 1.2m (4ft) away from the bowling crease and has a minimum length of 1.8m (6ft).

Return crease   These are at right angles to both ends of the bowling crease and extend behind it for at least 1.2m (4ft).

Round the wicket   When the bowler bowls the ball with his back to the stumps at the bowler's end.

Sight-screens   These are large, movable screens usually painted white or duck-egg blue and which are placed in line with the bowler's arm but behind the boundary so the batsman has a good sight of the ball.

Tail-enders   The players batting at Nos. 9, 10 and 11. They are usually the side's specialist bowlers and are not less esteemed for their lack of batting skill.

Taking guard   Making a mark on the batting crease so that the batsman knows where he is in relation to the stumps.

Tossing up   The captains meet before the game to ascertain who chooses whether to bat or field. The home captain tosses a coin and the away captain calls either heads or tails. The winner of the toss can then opt whether to field or bat first.

Wicket maiden   An over in which the bowler takes at least one wicket and concedes no runs.

Yorker   A bowling delivery which is pitched at the batsman's feet in the hope of passing under his bat.

INDEX